The Baseball Trivia Book To End All Baseball Trivia Books

The Baseball Trivia Book To End All Baseball Trivia Books

by

Bert Randolph Sugar

Freundlich Books
New York, New York

ISBN 0-88191-039-2

Published by Freundlich Books
(A division of Lawrence Freundlich Publications, Inc.)
212 Fifth Avenue
New York, N.Y. 10010

Distributed to the trade by The Scribner Book
Companies, Inc. 115 Fifth Avenue
New York, N.Y. 10003

Manufactured in the United States of America

10 9 8 7 6 5 4 3 2 1

DEDICATION

This book is lovingly dedicated to the memory of Bill Veeck, who taught us all that baseball was what it was originally meant to be: Fun.

Contents

Chapter 1 The Players 1
Chapter 2 The Batters 43
Chapter 3 The Pitchers 71
Chapter 4 The Hall of Fame 116
Chapter 5 The World Series 128
Chapter 6 The All Star Game 146
Chapter 7 The 7th Inning Stretch 157
Chapter 8 The Managers 185
Chapter 9 The Teams 194

INTRODUCTION
by Bert Randolph Sugar

The ninth decade of the twentieth century may well be remembered as the designer decade. We have designer jeans and designer water—Perrier. We also have designer exercises—aerobics. We have designer charities—Live Aid, Farm Aid, and every other manner of aid up to and excluding only Band Aid. Most significant to this book, we even have a designer game—Trivial Pursuit. The era of individual choice has been replaced by a programmed mind-set as frightening as anything conceived by Orwell. But then, Orwell never conceived of the day when Trivial Pursuit would be all the rage—especially the All-Star Sports Edition which not only mistakenly asks, "What four players wearing No. 44 hit 44 home runs in one year?" but also misspells this writer's name.

Trivial Pursuit is merely a 1980s formalization of the time-honored pastime of exchanging trivia—a word derived from the Latin word *trivium,* meaning "where three roads meet; the public square." Translated in the plural, it reads as, "street talk." In times of yore, religious contemplatives met in public squares by their favorite watering trough to argue esoteric issues such as how many angels can dance on the head of a pin. Today, the descendants of those contemplatives—now called fans—meet at modern watering holes—now called pubs or bars—to exchange their own esoterica: trivia.

The props for trivia are immutable and hallowed by tradition. But the variations are endless. There are the questions asked by those who call themselves members of the Baker Street Irregulars, read Sherlock Holmes fans. They pose such puzzlers as "What was the name of Mycroft's club?" Hint! Mycroft is Sherlock's brother.

And then there are those yuppies weaned on TV—that 23-inch magic lantern that transported more people to fantasyland than Aladdin's lamp—who have now joined in the trivia craze, transforming the cathode baby–sitters of their youth into street talk, or trivia. One such group are those who idolize Jackie Gleason and the *Honeymooners.* They pose such questions as, "Where is Ralph Kramden's building?", and answer something that sounds like Chauncey Street in the Bensonhurst section of Brooklyn, when any self–respecting Brooklynite worth his salted salami can tell you that Chauncey Street is located in Bushwick. But never mind. It's trivia, even if it's wrong trivia.

All of which serves merely as *hors d'oeuvres* for what has become trivia's *entrée*: baseball. For baseball not only possesses a rich fabric and texture conducive to trivia, but a mother lode of statistics that can be panned for diamond diamonds. And those who want their trivia 98 proof, at least those in and around New York, normally gravitate toward a place where baseball trivia is spoken fluently—even if those who speak it don't—Runyon's Saloon on East 50th Street, the baseball triviot's favorite watering hole.

It was there one night, on my diocesan rounds to treat the similarly sick and afflicted, that I found myself in the company of two baseball triviot's of the first water. And Scotch to boot. Allowing the questions to marinate slowly, along with everything else at the table, we soon found ourselves joined without so much as a, "How–do–you–do", by a couple of visiting firemen who had come to Runyon's in search of internal rubbing alcohol. Having spent their hard–earned Reagan dollars for drinks and the open bar offering of pretzels, the two had now chosen to partake of what they perceived as yet another open bar offering, a discussion of the deeper meaning of triviametrics taking place at our table.

We should have known better. It was like a priest inviting a few friends in to hear confessions as these lusty trenchermen became not only part and parcel of the conversation, but its luggage as well, freighting it with trivia questions that had us writhing in the aisles. Speaking in italics, their questions were skim milk posing as *créme de cacao*. One of their best, as I remember—but, then again, I was doing my damndest not to—had to do with, "The last man to have 100 RBIs in his first two full seasons in the majors?" It was answered by one of my tippling partners who didn't even pause in his fluid drinking motion: "Ray Jablonski." Their insults to the noble questions of fast–fading memory reminded me of the old man who had relieved himself in his blue serge suit: it had felt good, but nobody had noticed.

Almost as if on cue, and motivated by my vagrant thought that trivia is not much different than whiskey—one must pass off the worst and retain only the best—I asked permission to be excused, better to visit the facilities. Permission granted. There I might pick up a trivia pointer or two from the walls of Runyon's men's room. After all, hadn't Anthony Newley actually first seen that piece of graffito, "stop the world I want to get off," on P. J. Clarke's W. C. wall, and adopted it as the title of his Broadway show? It was then that what to my wandering eye should appear but the following legend framed on the wall above the booth, written by that poet laureate of the misbegotten, Dan Jenkins:

Stages of Drunkenness

1. Witty and charming
2. Rich and powerful
3. Philosophical
4. Against the S.S.T.

5. F— dinner
6. Witty and charming—Part II
7. For the S.S.T.
8. Tease the Giants and the over
9. Morose and despondent
10. Invisible
11. Bulletproof

Jenkins should have added yet another one of the rules of the house: never let a drunk catch your eye, especially one with baseball trivia to spare and to share.

Wandering back from the loo and giving wide berth to the corner table where the interlopers were now cruising on their batteries—and my two erstwhile tablemates were now trying mightily to yawn without opening their mouths, on the cusp of calling the game on account of lack of interest—I chanced to find myself in front of the jukebox which was belting out Billie Holliday's, "God Bless the Child." Comfortably bracing myself against the jukebox, I fumbled like Steve Sax trying to fish a quarter out of my pocket to play the overture from *Guys and Dolls* in honor of the spiritual, if not the actual, founder of Runyon's and I found myself again staring at the wall. And there, jumping out at me—which, by now, had become the dominant note of the evening—was a framed article from an ancient issue of *Inside Sports* entitled, "The Fan" and written by one of the two co–owners of Runyon's, Joe Healey. Now Healey and his partner, Jim Costello, have carried me longer than my mother, and I am fortunate to know them. Nevertheless, there are, as Winston Churchill was wont to say, taking pains never to end a sentence with a preposition, certain things, "up with which I will not put." And that is the lack of a sense of humor and fun, something that baseball trivia possesses in abundance. Properly constructed, baseball trivia is rococo. It begs for fanciful curved forms and ornamentation, not a denuded straight line that can best be described as question and answer.

"This article," the text begins with proper solemnity, "is dedicated to the three–sewer men of statistics, the triviacs.""Triviacs?" Indeed! What the hell is that? Hurrying on,

Healey, having only the ticket of admission and not yet paid his dues, adds, "They are the barroom bleacher bums who can go toe–to–toe or mouth–to–mouth with the best when it comes down to what year? And who was on deck?" Here I chance to leave out a reference to that Cleveland of sports trivia, football. Healey continues, "By their dedication and perseverance, they have exposed the lowest form of vermin—the spreader of bad trivia, that rotten apple who irresponsibly serves up the bad question and inaccurate answer. Bad trivia can be separated into two classifications: (1) The not–so–cute gimmick and (2) the not–so–obvious error."

Healey is only warming up now. "NSCG questions are an insult to the intelligence of our sect. Examples: who is the only person to play for the New York Knicks, the Brooklyn Dodgers, and the New York Rangers? Gladys Gooding, of course. She was the organist. This atrocious germ is still making the rounds." Forget the fact that Healey misspelled Ms. Goodding's name; he is making the case for critics, that band of hail fellows well crossed whom Nunally Johnson once called, "A fellow who despises you because you haven't got his talent." Nor has Mr. Healey Mr. Johnson's sense of humor either. Healey then throws in another of his pet peeves, "What brothers have combined to hit the most home runs in history?" He answers, "The Boyers? Sorry, Clete's 162 and big brother Ken's 282 put their figure at 444. The DiMaggios? Wrong again. Even though there were three of them, Joe's 361, Vince's 125 and Dom's 87 got them into second place with 573. The winners: the Aarons with 768. Hank supplied 98.3 percent of the work, hitting 755 homers, while Tommie had just 13." What pious twaddle, I thought, as I glanced back at two of Healey's most devout disciples still glued in place at my (former) table asking aged–in–the– woods questions like, "Who was the only man to pinch–hit for Ted Williams?" (Carroll Hardy), "Who threw the Called Shot to Babe Ruth?" (Presuming there *was* one, Charlie Root), and other bosh, *ad nauseum.*

"Alright, Mr. Healey, you have sown the wind, now reap the whirlwind," I muttered to no one in particular. Since both questions mentioned in Healey's framed manifesto (just 93 points shy on the over and under for Luther's theses, if you're counting) were contained in my first baseball trivia book, *Who was Herry Steinfeldt? And Other Baseball Trivia Questions,* I determined then and there to write yet another. One with humor and fun in it to give the lie to Mr. Healey's slander. And if Mr. Healey has to ask what fun baseball trivia is, then I would refer him to the man whose name now nestled just under my right elbow on his jukebox, Louie Armstrong. Armstrong, when asked to explain rhythm, said, "Man, if you gotta ask, you'll never know!"

Thus, the idea for *The Baseball Trivia Book to End All Baseball Trivia Books.* Its title may sound a little optimistic—even presumptuous—like doing a crossword puzzle in ink. However, since the issuance of my first baseball trivia book, *Who was Harry Steinfeldt?*—not incidentally, the first baseball trivia book ever published—the popularity of baseball trivia has rivaled that of interest rates on municipal bonds. And 1985 was a year when trivia became a current event, arguably the greatest year ever for trivia. A perfect time for baseball trivia redux.

In 1985 Pete Rose took a bat and dubbed himself the greatest hitter in the history of baseball. It was the year in which Tom Seaver and Rod Carew both made history by joining two exclusive clubs, the 300–win and 3,000–hit clubs, on the same day. This was the second time in history that two men joined the 300–win inner circle in one year. It was the year that Dwight Gooden, the youngest man ever to win the Cy Young Award and pitching's version of the Triple Crown, added as many epaulets to baseball's already encrusted history as he did to his own growing chevrons. And sprinkled throughout, like Easter eggs, were other trivia goodies: the fourth time in history that the World Series had been completely played in the central time zone; the first time a team in the Series had two 20–game winners, one batting champion, and a stolen–base champ; the second time in history two men were tagged out at the plate by the catcher in tandem; the year the youngest pitcher ever started a seventh game of the Series and to start two in any World Series; the year the all–time base–stealing record for a rookie was set—and on, and on.

It was also a year when past trivia and current events so

merged that Bobby Bonds got caught up in it. And in his mental underwear as well, claiming on a Miller Lite commercial that he had stolen 681 bases, when the actual number was inscribed in gravenstone as 461. The commercials were pulled, never to be seen again, a victim of bad trivia. Nineteen eighty–five was a helluva year for baseball trivia, and one heckuva year to write a book, . . . *To End All Baseball Trivia Books.*

Because baseball trivia is a look at the sport through a different looking glass, almost like the refraction one gets looking through the bottom of an empty highball glass, great care and feeding was devoted to presenting trivia–cum–history that would combine the good old days in golden–oldie questions, with some up–to–date questions—remembering always that today will become the good–old–days tomorrow—and a few mix–and–match matings that combine the eras in a you–can't–look–it–up manner. Then, there are the never–thought–of before questions. Even if they have some gimmickry added as a sprightly garnish. Mix them all up, properly freshen them every now and then, stir and serve. You now have a frothy concoction, a book version of the old watering hole, "where the three roads meet" and only street talk is spoken.

If you're still with me, here are a few words about the question–and–answer approach taken here. Or, rather, the non–question–and–answer approach. The traditional Q&A trivia book requires more thumbs than the average person possesses to hold the reader's place at the question page while he struggles to open the answer page, all the while trying not to see the next 10 or so answers below. I am reminded of the multiple choice answer I once ran across back in some college course or other although the question has now faded far from memory. The answer was, "(A) Euripides; (B) Eumenides; (C) All of these; (D) None of these." I've eschewed that format in favor of one that I believe is more fun—with answers within answers, almost like the old Christmas balls made up of ribbons that would produce more and more gifts the more they were unwound. I can only hope the reader has as much fun reading the answers as I had constructing them.

Because the making of *The Baseball Trivia Book to End All Base-*

ball Trivia Books either necessitated my holding daily seances with the dead shades of Alexander Cartwright, Grantland Rice, and Judge Kenesaw Mountain Landis, or the live wires who frequent the booths at Runyon's and provide me with companionship and comfort in my hours of need, I opted for the latter. Seeing that some of my questions looked like an unfinished German sentence, the verb tossed in at the end for meaning, they somehow, someway, somewhere transformed my trivia into something fathomable. To them I am indebted and would like to proffer each and every a hearty, Salute!" Failing that, can only offer them public thanks. Those who helped this book take flight and fancy include a team which for want of a better phrase I'll call my, Trivia Swat Team. The first group I'll call my bench: Ev Cope, Chuck Singer, Karen Cerrone, Phil Corper, Gregg Small, Dick Cohen, Nora MacKenzie, Bob Davids, Larry Freundlich, Allen Barra, Christie James, Ross Adell, Steve Nadel, Bob O'Brien, Charles Jay, Early Wynn, Rip Sewell, Carl Furillo—and even, yes! Joe Healey. My starting team includes Chuck Covello, Tom Heitz, Rick Cerrone, and David Neft, plus a tip of the Sugar hat to baseball's premier cartoonist, Bill Gallo. And my three superstars; Red Foley of the New York *Daily News,* Scott Flatow of SABR, and John Grabowski of the *Baseball Trivia Newsletter* (217 Crystal Avenue, New York, 10302). As a conglomerate they are proof positive that baseball trivia wears no one man's collar, but belongs to all—especially to you, the fan.

Bert Randolph Sugar
Runyon's, January 3, 1986

1st Inning
The Players

WHO WAS THE ONLY MAN TO GET TWO HITS IN TWO GAMES IN TWO CITIES FOR TWO DIFFERENT TEAMS ON THE SAME DAY?

Bill Veeck once considered trading Norm Cash from the White Sox to the Yankees for infielder Andy Carey, mischievously envisioning headlines which would read "Cash and Carey." But that trade always remained one of Bill's delicious jokes that never materialized. One that did, however, rivaled it for its singularity: trading two players from opposing teams between games in a doubleheader so that they could confront each other in the second game wearing new uniforms. Between games of a morning–afternoon doubleheader on May 30, 1922, outfielder Cliff Heathcote of the Chicago Cubs was traded to the St. Louis Cardinals for outfielder Max Flack of the Cards. Each had gotten hits in the morning portion of the doubleheader, but neither would get a hit for his new club in the afternoon game.

The only man who *did* get two hits in two games for two different teams—and in two different cities as well—was Joel Youngblood, who, on August 4, 1982, hit a two–run single for the New York Mets in the third inning of a game at Chicago against the Cubs. Told he had been traded to Montreal for pitcher Tom Gorman, Youngblood raced to Chicago's O'Hare Airport to catch a plane to Philadelphia. He joined his new club just in time to be inserted into the line–up as a defensive replacement in the outfield. Later he would come to bat and get a hit off Phillies pitcher Steve Carlton to participate in baseball's rarest single–day club quinella. Also, by facing Carlton in his second game and the Cubs' Ferguson Jenkins in his first game, Youngblood is the only player ever to face two pitchers with 3,000 strikeouts in one day.

WHAT BALLPLAYER HOLDS THE RECORD FOR HITTING INTO THE MOST TRIPLE PLAYS?

Rare is the player who hits into even one triple play during his entire career. Some who have have made that one a memorable one. Like Kansas City's "Whitey" Herzog, who hit into the only all-Cuban triple play in history (courtesy of Senors Pascual, Becquer and Valdivielso). Or San Diego's Dave Cash, who hit into the only all-rookie triple play (aided and abetted by Messrs. Pettini, Sularz and Murray). Or the Braves' Leo Foster, who, in his first game in the majors, began his career by hitting into one. Or the Mets' Joe Pignatano, who, in his final big-league at bat wrote *finis* to his career by hitting into one. Pignatano's manager, Casey Stengel, could only shake his head and mumble, "We've got to learn how to stay out of those triple plays." But one man who never quite learned how "to stay out of those triple plays" was Baltimore Oriole third baseman Brooks Robinson, who cornered the market on them, hitting into four during his career. Robinson thus proved that he could do anything—including hitting into triple plays—better than anyone else.

TRIPLE PLAYS HIT INTO BY BROOKS ROBINSON

DATE	OPPONENTS	FIELDERS & POSITIONS	INNING
June 2, 1958	Washington	Bridges (SS)–Becquer (1B)	6
Sept. 10, 1964	Washington	Kennedy (SS)–Blasinggame (2B)—Cunningham (1B)–Brumley (C)	5
Aug. 18, 1965	Boston	Malzone (3B)–Mantilla (2B)—Horton (1B)–Malzone (3B)	1
Aug. 6, 1967	Chicago	K. Boyer (3B)–Buford (2B)—McCraw (1B)	5

WHO IS THE ONLY PLAYER TO TWICE BE A 3,000TH STRIKEOUT VICTIM?

Only nine pitchers have ever passed the 3,000–strikeout milestone; only one man has helped make history twice—Cesar Geronimo. Geronimo, playing for the Cincinnati Reds on July 17, 1974, was the 3,000th victim of St. Louis Cardinal great Bob Gibson, the second man—after Walter Johnson—to register 3,000 strikeouts. And then, on July 4, 1980, Geronimo made history of a reverse sort by becoming the 3,000th–strikeout victim of the man who would go on to become baseball's all–time leader—Nolan Ryan.

Other strike–out victims who have served as the unwitting catalysts to the greatness of others are: Rich Reese, Nolan Ryan's 383rd; Dick Williams, Tom Cheney's 21st; and Andre Dawson, Steve Carlton's 19th.

4

WHO WAS THE ONLY PLAYER TO PLAY HIS ENTIRE MAJOR LEAGUE CAREER FOR THREE TEAMS, IN THREE DIFFERENT LEAGUES, ALL IN ONE CITY?

Once upon a time, back in the dim, distant past, baseball's menu was made up of a surprising smorgasboard of leagues, making it all the easier for players to jump from league-to-league without ever having to leave their house. Especially if their umbilicus was to the city where they lived rather than to their team. Or league. Several Hall of Famers thus changed leagues almost as easily as they did suits of clothes, with Wilbert Robinson and John McGraw playing for three different Baltimore teams in three different leagues, Pud Galvin playing for three different Pittsburgh teams—which back then didn't have an "H" to hiss in—in three different leagues and King Kelly and Dan Brouthers playing for three Boston teams in three different leagues. However, each and every one of those three-timing greats *also* played for at least one other team in one other city. It remained for the man whose name appears last in the alphabetized listing of players in the Official Encyclopedia of Baseball, Edward "Dutch" Zwilling, to become the first—and only—player to play for three teams in three different leagues in one city. Zwilling spent his entire career in the city of Chicago, playing for the Chicago White Sox in the American League, the Chicago Whales in the Federal League and the Chicago Cubs in the National League—all in but four short years, ending in 1916. The last man in the alphabetized listing also shares something in common with the first man listed alphabetically in the Official Baseball Encyclopedia, Haron Aaron: Both led their league in home runs and RBI's.

WHO IS THE ONLY PLAYER TO PLAY IN ALL FOUR OF BASEBALL'S DIVISIONS IN ONE YEAR?

A player who senses he's about to be traded is like someone waiting in line for a taxicab to take him to whatever destination fate and the general manager dictate. In 1977 Dave Kingman, who, in the words of broadcaster Al Michaels, "played the outfield the way you'd figure Steve Martin would play *Hamlet,*" needed a whole fleet of taxicabs as he hopscotched his way throughout baseball's four divisions. He played for the New York Mets in the National League East, the San Diego Padres in the National League West, the California Angels in the American League West, and the New York Yankees in the American League East. Despite being part gypsy and part suitcase, Kingman still managed to hit a total of 26 homers, the most ever by a player on more than two teams in a season. But even the globetrotting Kingman has to share billing with Dick Williams who is the only manager to manage teams in each of baseball's four divisions: the Boston Red Sox in the American League East; the Oakland A's and the California Angels in the American League West; the Montreal Expos in the National League East; and the San Diego Padres in the National League West. Ironically, despite their checkered and almost checker–like careers, these two happy wanderers have never been in the same place at the same time.

WHO WAS THE FIRST FIRST BASEMAN TO HAVE THREE ASSISTS IN ONE INNING?

Pittsburgh Pirate manager Danny Murtaugh, upon hearing the public address announcement at Forbes Field that anyone interfering with a ball in play would be ejected from the ballpark, was heard to remark to anyone within earshot, "I hope Dick Stuart doesn't think that means him."

And for most of his 10–year career, Stuart seemed intent upon inflicting serious injury upon himself with a baseball glove. But it wasn't his glove that earned him his ticket to the majors; it was his bat. Brought up by the Pirates after hitting 66 home runs for the Lincoln, Neb. team in the Class A Western League in 1956, Stuart became the first man to hit 30 or more homers in each league. He hit a high of 35 for the Pirates in 1961 and 42 for the Red Sox in 1963.

However, no bevy, school, or clutch of homers could take the fans' collective minds off of Stuart's inept fielding, fielding that was so bad it earned him the title "Dr. Strangeglove" as he set the major–league mark for most times leading his league in errors at first base. He either led or tied in seven of his first nine years. But for one shining year, 1963, he somehow, someway figured out what to do with the glove that most people thought should have been bronzed. That year he led American League first basemen in putouts and assists, causing many to wonder if their confidence in Gibraltar was misplaced. And on the afternoon of June 28, 1963, he set the all–time record by assisting in all three of the first–inning outs, a rare feat for a man who had always fielded as if he had two left feet. It was equaled by Andre Thornton of the Cubs on August 22, 1975 and by Jim Maler of the Mariners in 1982, but it can never be surpassed, not as long as there are only three outs in an inning.

WHO WAS THE ONLY ROOKIE OF THE YEAR TO WIN THE AWARD ON A TEAM OTHER THAN THE ONE HE ORIGINALLY CAME UP WITH?

Of the 78 players selected by the Baseball Writers as Rookies of the Year, each one but one has won the award as a member of the team with which he first entered the majors. The one exception is Lou Piniella, the American League Rookie of the Year Award in 1969. Before Piniella won the 1969 Award, he had been a baseball nomad, wandering down the highways and byways of America in search of a landing spot. We won't follow his every move, but instead pick him up signing with Cleveland in 1962. Piniella was then drafted by Washington later that same year, was traded to Baltimore in '64, returned yet agan to Cleveland in a 1966 deal, and was drafted by Seattle in the 1968 expansion draft. Then jump cut to his trade to Kansas City in the spring of 1969, his sixth Major League organization. It was there in 1969 that Piniella found himself, both as a Royal and as a batter, compiling a .282 batting average and winning the Rookie of the Year Award—on a team other than the one he originally came up with.

WHAT CATCHER HOLDS THE RECORD FOR GIVING UP THE MOST STOLEN BASES IN ONE GAME?

Early in his managerial career one Wesley Branch Rickey, a highly religious man who refused to play ball or manage on Sundays, told his assembled troops, "Thou shalt not steal. I mean defensively. On offense, indeed thou shall steal. And thou must." Unfortunately, on the afternoon of June 28, 1907, the Washington Senators took the young New York Highlander catcher at his word and put him through one of the most humiliating days any catcher ever experienced. The Senators picked him clean, taking everything but his wallet as no less than 13 Washington base runners stole on him. He set an all–time record for catcher futility. It was enough to make most grown men cry. And a smart man like Rickey quit, which is exactly what he did. Returning to law school from which he graduated before resurfacing in 1913 as the manager of the lowly St. Louis Browns, he was one of six managers to possess an LL.B. along with their School of Hard Knocks diploma. John Montgomery Ward, Miller Huggins, Hughie Jennings, Muddy Ruel, and Tony La Russa were the others. Ironically, Rickey would remain in baseball for almost the next half century, enough time to witness history of a sort repeat itself 50 years after he had been personally victimized as the 1957 Senators stole 13 bases, the same number they had stolen against him. This time, though, the figure was for an entire year, a record for futility all its own.

WHO PLAYED CENTER FIELD FOR THE CLEVELAND INDIANS THE DAY BOB FELLER THREW HIS NO–HITTER AGAINST THE YANKEES?

Someone once asked Cleveland Indian pitcher Bob Lemon if pitching was his preference to which he replied, "No, give me the outfield. I want to be in there playing every day." Playing every day was a natural desire for Lemon who had originally earned his promotion to the majors as an everyday player, spending four years in the Cleveland farm system as a third baseman with an overall .287 average. However, the majors were a different cup of tea, and Lemon was not to be added to the Indians roster after his dismal one–for–nine showing in his first two major league tryouts with the Tribe. Seeking an alternative route to the big leagues after the end of World War II, Lemon tried his hand at pitching even though he had but a mere two innings of mound experience in the minors. He went to the mound 32 times in his first full year, 1946, and pitched creditably, posting a 4–5 won–lost record and a 2.49 Earned Run Average. Nevertheless, Lemon still yearned to play every day. Manager Lou Boudreau let him play in the outfield on spot occasions in place of centerfielder Pat Seerey, who was on his way to leading the American League in strikeouts.

And so it was that on the afternoon of April 30, 1946 Lemon could be found in the starting Indian lineup as centerfielder when Bob Feller pitched a no–hitter against the New York Yankees, the second of his three no–hitters. The losing Yankees pitcher that afternoon? It was Floyd "Bill" Bevens, who would lose his own bid for a no–hitter the next year in the 1947 World Series, his last appearance in the major leagues.

Eleven years later Lemon would find himself in yet another bit role, this time coming on in relief with two out in the first to spell Herb Score against the Yankees after Score was felled by Gil McDougald's linedrive. Lemon would win that May 7, 1957 game, 2–1.

WHO WAS THE ONLY PLAYER TO BE THROWN OUT OF A MAJOR LEAGUE GAME BUT NEVER PLAY IN ONE?

On September 27, 1951, the Brooklyn Dodgers were playing the Braves in Boston, trying mightily to protect their fast–shrinking lead over the onrushing New York Giants, who, catching them in their stretch drive, forced the memorable play–off series won by Bobby Thomson's "Shot Heard 'Round the World." With the score 3–3 in the bottom of the eighth, Jackie Robinson cleanly fielded a ground ball and fired it home to catcher Roy Campanella in an attempt to get the onrushing Brave base runner, outfielder Bob Addis, at the plate. But plate umpire, Frank Dascoli, called Addis "safe" with the Braves' fourth—and winning—run. An argument ensued as the Dodgers took more than minor issue with the call. First Campanella, then coach Cookie Lavagetto and finally the entire Dodger bench joined in. Finally, Dascoli had had enough. Unable to find the ringleaders on the bench, he ordered a mass evacuation, throwing out the entire Dodger bench.

One of those cleared out of the Dodgers' dugout by Dascoli was a young outfielder named Bill Sharman, just called up by the Dodgers from Ft. Worth where he had hit a respectable .286. Sharman, who would later go on to basketball fame with the Boston Celtics—setting many NBA free–throw records during his career—would never appear in a major league game. He completed his baseball career the following year playing with St. Paul of the American Association. Granted that throwing out Sharman was like blaming the Johnstown flood on a leaky toilet in Harrisburg, his ouster became an interesting footnote to baseball history: the only player ever to be thrown out of a major league game without having played in one.

WHO ARE THE ONLY THREE PLAYERS IN MAJOR-LEAGUE HISTORY TO PLAY 1,000 OR MORE GAMES AT TWO DIFFERENT POSITIONS?

In Greek Mythology, there were nine muses. In folklore, the tale goes that a cat has nine lives. And, in baseball, a team has nine men at nine different positions. Not seven, but nine. Why this seemingly minor point is being belabored here is because so many men who should know better have seen fit to lump all three outfield positions into just one, leaving record-keepers with the impression that a baseball team is made up of just seven positions, not one. That's hardly what Alexander Cartwright had in mind lo those many years ago when he first laid down the working outline of what was to become our National Pastime. And it's not what Bob Davids, the keeper of Mr. Cartwright's flame and baseball statistician extraordinaire, had in mind when he went through the time-honored statistics with a sophistication heretofore unknown to find those who had played 1,000 or more games at two different positions—dividing the outfield into three parts, like Gaul: left, right and center.

Forget the fact that Pete Rose, after signing his original multimillion dollar contract with the Phillies, was heard to exclaim, "With all the money I'm making, I should be playing two positions." For although Mr. Rose played several positions, all well thank you!, he never played 1,000 games at two positions. Nor did two of those who are often credited with having accomplished the feat, again counting the outfield as three positions: Stan Musial and Ron Fairly—Musial playing 1,016 games at first, 907 games in left, 299 in center and 699 in right; and Fairly playing 1,218 games at first, 211 in left, 103 in center and 728 in right, oftimes changing outfield positions during the same game. According to Davids, the only three Colosseus to straddle two different positions for 1,000 or more games are: Ernie Banks, who played 1,125 games at short and another 1,259 at first: Rod Carew, who, through 1985, had played 1,130 games at second and another 1,184 at first; and George Herman Ruth, who was continually babied by the Yankees, being moved away from the "Sun Field," lest his scalloped and heavily indented exterior take on the look of a beached and bleached whale—Ruth playing 1,054 games in left and another 1,133 in right, Yankee Stadium's non-"Sun Field."

WHO WAS THE ONLY MAN IN BASEBALL HISTORY TO PLAY EXACTLY 1,000 GAMES FOR ONE TEAM AND HAVE EXACTLY 1,000 BASE HITS?

One of baseball's most intriguing subtexts is the numerical symmetry to be found in its never–ending statistics. For instance, Joe DiMaggio's incredible hit streak shows DiMaggio hitting 56 singles and scoring 56 runs over 56 games. And Stan Musial's 3,630 hits can be broken down into 1,815 hits at home and 1,815 hits away. Others that crop up include Bibb Falk's five hits, five RBI's and five runs scored in the first five innings of a 1930 game against the Philadelphia A's; Sandy Koufax's 223 strikeouts in 223 innings in 1964; and Phil Cavaretta's retirement in 1951 after having played 1,951 games for the Chicago Cubs. There is even the statistical coincidence of Dazzy Vance, who over his entire playing career was paid $197,000 and had—you guessed it!—197 wins. But perhaps the most intriguing of all symmetrical questions is answered by the career of Joe Gordon who played exactly 1,000 games for the New York Yankees from 1938 through 1946 (with time out during World War II) and had exactly 1,000 hits. Gordon, who would go on to play another 566 games for the Cleveland Indians, won the American League Most Valuable Player Award in 1942 despite leading the league in errors, strikeouts, and double plays—also a one–of–a–kind.

WHO WON THE STOLEN BASE CHAMPIONSHIP WITH THE LEAST NUMBER OF STOLEN BASES IN ONE YEAR?

By the late 1940s the stolen base had fallen into disuse and disrepute, moved to the back of baseball's bus by the over-emphasis on power baseball. The base–stealing totals plummeted faster than the stock market did on October 29, 1929. By

1950 the total for the entire American League was 278, less than the all–time mark for a single season by one club—the 1911 Giants who stole 347 bases, two of which were even stolen by their mascot, Charlie "Victory" Faust.

The year 1950 saw Dom DiMaggio lead the league in stolen bases with but 15, the least number of stolen bases ever to lead a league. When one of the members of the New York chapter of something called the BLOHARDS—an acronym which stands for the "Benevolent and Loyal Order of the Honorable and Ancient Red Sox Die–Hard Sufferers"—moved on unsteady feet over to DiMaggio and proceeded to put both in mouth, asking him how he came to lead the league with 15 stolen bases in 1950, Dom could only smile and say, "Pesky missed the hit–and–run sign that many times."

WHAT PLAYER ACTIVELY PLAYED DURING THE TERMS OF THE MOST AMERICAN PRESIDENTS?

The dictionary is a wonderful guide to the correct spelling of words which can be located only if one knows how to spell them correctly in the first place. Or in the second place. One of those which can be spelled on a sometime basis is the word "longevity," which Mister Webster in his infinite wisdom and in his definitive tome defines as, "long duration, as in an occupation . . . ." Throughout baseball's long and illustrious history, several players have also enjoyed a long and illustrious history, or "longevity," including 55 non–pitchers who played 20 or more years in the majors and another 28 pitchers.

However, an even tighter little island are those players who played during the course of four decades, the "Four–Decade Player," as he has become known. The year 1960 saw a brace of three players whose careers had all started in 1939 and who, as the new season started, moved into their fourth decade: Mickey

Vernon, Ted Williams, and Early Wynn. They would be joined on September 11, 1976 when Orestes "Minnie" Minoso came back for three games, as much waiting to hear the echoes of an earlier day, an earlier day that would never be heard again as to qualify for membership into the exclusive "Four–Decade" club. Minoso, who would go on to appear twice at the plate in 1980, added yet another decade to his already crowded escutcheon. But one man who came up in 1939 didn't qualify although he played into 1960. He was Elmer Valo. Valo was brought up in the closing weeks of the 1939 season by Connie Mack for an appraisal and sat on the Philadelphia A's bench game after game awaiting his chance to prove himself. Finally, on the last day of the season, Mack sent him in as a pinch hitter and Valo wrangled a walk. But a diligent scorekeeper, one Red Smith of the local Philadelphia *Record,* a then–going concern, pointed out to Mack that because the youngster hadn't officially been signed to a contract, the A's, and Mack personally, were subject to a fine at the hands of the commissioner. Smith therefore requested permission to leave Valo's name out of the official box score, a conscious omission that cost Valo his chance for trivia immortality.

As the 1980s turned the corner, acting as a portculus dropping down on one age and opening the way into yet another one, three more players joined the club, bringing its total membership to 18 card–carrying members: Jim O'Rourke (1876-1904); Dan Brouthers (1879-1904); Jack O'Connor (1887-1910); William J. "Kid" Gleason (1888-1912); Deacon Jim McGuire (1884-1912); John B. Ryan (1889-1913); Eddie Collins (1906-1930); Nick Altrock (1898-1933); Jack Quinn (1909-1933); Louis Norman "Bobo" Newsom (1929-1953); Mickey Vernon (1939-1960); Ted Williams (1939-1960); Elmer Valo (1939-1961); Early Wynn (1939-1963); "Minnie" Minoso (1949-1980); Tim McCarver (1959-1980); Willie McCovey (1959-1980); and Jim Kaat (1959-1983).

Somewhere amongst those 18 players is the one who actively played during the terms of more American presidents than any other. The operative word here is "actively," a game–a–year not a season making. Deacon Jim McGuire played one game as a catcher for the 1904 New York Giants. Granted it was the pennant–clinching game, and further than that it gave the man who had the first National League hit back in 1876 the most years of service in the majors with 26; but he doesn't qualify as someone who was playing "actively," even if he did play—albeit on a nonactive basis—during the terms of seven U. S. presidents. Another who played during the terms of seven U. S. presidents was Nick Altrock. However, one can hardly call it "actively" as Altrock was merely called off the coaching lines and ceremonially trotted out like the queen's jewels to pinch-hit just four times in 101 years, his comebacks rivaling Frank Sinatra's in number. The man who *actively* played during the terms of more American presidents than any other player in major league history was the most recently retired four–decader. Jim Kaat, who "actively" played during the administrations of Eisenhower, Kennedy, Johnson, Nixon, Ford, Carter, and Reagan, the all-time record.

WHO WAS ON THE FIELD FOR BOTH HANK AARON'S RECORD-BREAKING GAME AND FOR PETE ROSE'S RECORD-BREAKING GAME?

Baseball's two most famous career records were Babe Ruth's 714 home runs and Ty Cobb's 4,191 base hits, thought by generations to be part of baseball's indestructible legend—Rocks of Gibraltar which, along with Lou Gehrig's playing streak and Joe DiMaggio's hitting streak, would stand for all time. But on the evening of April 8, 1974, Hank Aaron shattered one of those Rocks driving a fastball thrown by Los Angeles Dodger pitcher Al Downing into the bullpen for the 715th home run of his long, long career. As Aaron leaped around the bases and the scoreboard in Atlanta Stadium electronically signaled "715," he raced past first baseman Steve Garvey of the Los Angeles Dodgers who shouted out his congratulations, a tribute that was drowned out by the sound of 53,775 voices all shouting their hosannas to the new king of the home–run hill in one voice. Eleven years later the also seemingly unbreakable record of Ty Cobb cracked under the constant pressure of Pete Rose who made his 4,192nd base hit on the afternoon of September 11, 1985 against the San Diego Padres. As Rose raced down to first in the breakneck style he had patented, who was there to greet him but the Padres first baseman, Steve Garvey, this time making sure his congratulations were heard above the crowd.

WHO IS THE ONLY MAJOR LEAGUE CENTER FIELDER EVER TO CATCH A FOUL BALL?

Many swiftfooted center fielders have been given the added burden of covering left and right fields as well for outfielders whose movements look as if they were chained to Morpheus's slow carriage. One such was Frankie Baumholtz, who played center for the Chicago Cubs between the twin towers of Ralph Kiner and Hank Sauer, hardly two merchants of velocity. During the year–and–a–half Baumholtz provided the mortar to this outfield suffering from feet of clay—Kiner and Sauer both shouting, "It's all yours, Frankie," or "lots of room, Frankie,"—he was officially dubbed, "The bravest center fielder of all time" by one Chicago sportswriter.

Another was the anchor of the accident known as the 1962 New York Mets' outfield (such as it was), Richie Ashburn. Ashburn was in the Mets' starting lineup on their very first day in history, April 11, 1962, between right fielder Gus Bell and left fielder Frank Thomas. They were joined on April 25th by shortstop Elio Chacon. On more than one occasion, Ashburn, calling for the ball in the traditional, "I've got it," would find Elio Chacon, who didn't understand English, banging into him. Not wanting to spend the entire season sitting home watching his bones mend, Ashburn finally arranged a set of signals with Chacon that would have him call out, *"Yo lo tengo"* so that the Spanish–speaking shortstop would comprendo and pull up short of a collision. The first time Ashburn camped out under a tall fly, he shouted out the agreed–upon, *"Yo lo tengo"* to wave off Chacon, only to find himself in a collision with Thomas who didn't understand Spanish. Ashburn hung up his spikes and bandages at the end of the year rather than risk another year of playing bumper cars.

However, the one center fielder who managed the almost impossible was another speed merchant, Johnny Mostil, who played centerfield for the Chicago White Sox in the 1920s. Mostil led the American League in stolen bases twice, in runs once, in putouts twice, in total chances–per–game three times in, and fielding average once—attesting to both his agility and his ability. His left fielder was Bibb Falk, who, during an exhibition game in Nashville's Sulphur Dell ballpark, a vest–pocket park where anything was within reach, was communing with nature when one of the opposing team hit a high, looping foul. Mostil, sensing that Falk had better things to do than pursue the ball, sprinted past the foul line, and running three furlongs in front of the ball the whole way, lunged into the stands after the ball, coming up with the only putout ever registered by a major league center fielder.

NAME THE LAST SET OF TWINS TO PLAY IN THE MAJORS.

Statistically, twins occur approximately once in every 80 to 87 births. But, of the 13,000 men who have played major league baseball since the year Zip, only eight sets of twins can be counted amongst their number, less than one–twentieth the statistical probability of twins playing baseball. And while there must be some argument to counter these numbers—but without any relevant facts to contradict the figures at hand—it can only be assumed that the lack of twins stems from baseball's abhorrence of doubleheaders.

The first wombmates on the baseball scene were John and Phillip Reccius, born, ironically, under the sign of Gemini, the Twins, on June 7, 1862. The Reccius Brothers both came up to Louisville in the old American Association in 1882. They put in a total of 10 years between them, with a combined batting average of .228 and a pitching record of 10 wins and 18 losses. The second set was the Hunters, George and Bill, who roamed the outfields for Cleveland and Brooklyn for three short years in the first decade of the twentieth century. They batted a combined total of .208. The third set was Ray and Roy Grimes, the two putting in seven years—six of which were Ray's—in the 1920s. Together they batted .322, the highest total for any of the eight sets.

The Shannons, Joe and Red, were born two years after the Grimes, but debuted a full five years before, both coming up with the Boston Braves of 1915. Joe was never heard of again, but Red played for seven years during the 1920s and, largely through his efforts, gave the duo a combined batting average of .258. The Jonnard Brothers, Bubber and Claude, a pitcher–catcher duo, put in a combined 12 years, longest total period for any of the double takes, and had a total average of .230 (for Bubber, the catcher) and 14 wins and 12 losses (for Claude, the only twin ever to appear in more than one World Series, seeing action for the 1923 and 1924 Giants, both in losing causes).

It was to be another thirty years until the next set of twins saw the light of day and the Majors as well, this time in the double–play combination of Eddie and Johnny O'Brien. They spent a total of 11 years with that woeful collection of athletes known as the Pittsburgh Pirates of the 1950s—a team that had driven manager Billy Meyer to scream, "You clowns could go on *What's My Line* in your uniforms and stump the panel." Together, the O'Briens batted .245 and, trying their dual hands on the mound, had a 2–3 record. The next to last set of twin brothers were the Edwards, Marshall and Mike, who played a total of six years between them, batted a combined average of .252, with Marshall playing in the 1982 World Series for Milwaukee.

The last set of twins to play in the majors was the Cliburn Brothers, Stan and Stew, yet another brother pitcher–catcher act. The Cliburns surfaced in 1980 (Stan) and 1984 (Stew) and only Stew still remains on the scene, a pitcher for the California Angels, one–half of the last of eight sets of twins to play in the Major Leagues.

WHO WAS THE YOUNGEST PLAYER EVER TO PLAY MAJOR LEAGUE BASEBALL?

Common wisdom would have it that the youngest ballplayer ever to appear in a major league game was Cincinnati Reds pitcher, Joe Nuxhall, who, just seven weeks shy of his 16th birthday, came in to relieve against the league–leading St. Louis Cardinals on June 10, 1944 and was rewarded for his efforts with five Cardinal runs on two hits and five bases on balls in two–thirds of an inning. But common wisdom hardly being the currency one can bank, or bank on, Nuxhall's claim to fame must be included with those covered by George Gershwin's song, "It Ain't Necessarily So."

For the real honor goes to a man–child named Fred Chapman who toiled in those days before the enactment of child labor laws. All that had been known about Master Chapman could have been written on a postcard crowded with a description of the awful scene on the reverse side, there being more than enough room left over for an oversized postage stamp. But that was before we went to that final repository of baseball history, the Hall of Fame Library in Cooperstown, N.Y. There librarian

Tom Heitz unearthed the following small bits of information on Master Chapman from his skimpy biographical folder bedecked by the dust of the ages. He was born on November 24, 1872, according to a photo showing the birthdate on his tombstone in the Evergreen Cemetery in Union City, Pa. He died on December 14, 1957, a fact contained in his obit in the Union City newspaper. And he appeared in a game on Friday, July 22, 1887, as chronicled in a yellowing newspaper box score of the time—in a game between the Athletics of Philadelphia and Cleveland, in which Chapman, in the quaint newspaper language of yesteryear, "officiated," to be read "pitched." The game was a forfeit 9–0 win for Philadelphia, occasioned by an interference call against Cleveland on an attempted double steal by outfielder Harry Stovey and second baseman Lou Bierbauer, meaning that all records go into the record books except the pitcher's, thus giving Chapman an 0–0 record with a complete game in his only appearance as the youngest player ever.

Even Chapman was an elder statesman, however, when it came to being the youngest player in the history of organized ball. In 1931, at the tender young age of 13, Joe Schultz, the son of former major leaguer Joe Schultz, Sr. and himself a future major league player and manager, came to bat as a pinch hitter for the Houston team his father ran.

However, eclipsing even the marks of Chapman and Schultz was a 12–year–old batboy for the Fitzgerald team in the Georgia State League named Charles Relford, who stood less than a hand higher than the bats he handled. With the local Fitzgerald team on the losing end of a 13–0 score, the crowd, such as it was, began derisively chanting, "Put in the batboy." Manager Charles Ridgeway consulted the home plate umpire and then, without further ado, sent in the batboy to bat. Relford grounded sharply to third base and, in the top of the ninth, went to center field, where he handled one ball cleanly and made a sensational catch of a sinking line drive. Not incidentally, Relford, who was black, broke the color barrier in the league and in the state as well.

WHO WAS THE ONLY MAN TO PLAY IN BABE RUTH'S LAST YEAR AND IN HANK AARON'S FIRST YEAR?

Babe Ruth ended his playing career by appearing in 28 games for the 1935 Boston Braves, his greatness compromised dearly by age, a mere memory of what he once was. One of those players who witnessed firsthand the last few days of an institution, one who, in fact, now moved more like an institution than a player, was the Chicago Cubs' first baseman, Phil Cavarretta, who had come up the previous year, 1934, as an 18–year–old rookie direct from Chicago's Lane Tech. Cavarretta would play for the Cubs through 1953 and then move over to the crosstown Chicago White Sox, where he would play through 1955. Thus, he was the only player to be able to lay claim to having been active during Babe Ruth's last year and Hank Aaron's first year. Cavarretta, himself, admitted he never played against Ruth, witnessing the end of a great career from the bench; and, of course, he played for the White Sox during Aaron's first two years and so never played directly against Aaron. Nevertheless, he was active during both careers, being only one of a small group of players who spanned eras. Pete Rose is the only batter to face both Sandy Koufax and Dwight Gooden, and Al Benton the only pitcher to face both Babe Ruth and Mickey Mantle.

WHO WAS THE LAST MAN TO CATCH BABE RUTH AND THE ONLY MAN TO CATCH TED WILLIAMS IN THE MAJORS?

Brooklyn sportswriter Tommy Holmes was once moved to comment, "Some 20 years ago I stopped talking about the Babe for the simple reason that I realized those who had never seen him wouldn't believe me." Ruth brought glamour back into the sordidness of besmirched baseball, suffering through the revelations of the Black Sox scandal of 1919 and proving to be its savior—his parabolic blasts rewriting the record book and his presence producing attendance figures that looked like World War I body counts. But his whole was greater than the sum of his mammoth parts. Before his bat saved the National Pastime, Ruth had been a great pitcher, one who had more victories for a left–hander at the age of 23 than anyone presently enshrined in the Hall of Fame. And it was not without more than some small sense of pride that this man who could strut sitting down, puffed himself up like a pouter pigeon when dwelling on his favorite achievement, his 29⅔ consecutive scoreless innings pitched in World Series competition.

Nearing the end of his long and glorious career, Ruth would occasionally take the mound not only to try to wash away the improbability of the calendar, but also to remind the fans of his once greatness, even if his actions on the mound were only a memory of that greatness. No less than four times after he came to the Yankees in 1920, he took the mound, all four times he won. The last time was a nine-inning complete game on October 1, 1933 against the Red Sox, appropriately throwing in a home run to win, 6–5. His catcher that day was Joe Glenn, then catching only his fifth game of the season and the 11th of his career. Glenn's career would continue for six more years on a part–time basis, including the afternoon of August 24, 1940, when, in his last Major League game, he caught two innings pitched by Ted Williams in his one and only pitching appearance in professional baseball. That afternoon Williams pitched only two innings against the American League pennant winners, the Detroit Tigers, giving up three hits and no bases on balls and recording one strikeout against Tiger first baseman Rudy York.

WHAT TWO PLAYERS WITH 400 OR MORE HOMERS STOLE HOME 10 TIMES OR MORE?

When one thinks of the theft of home—a singular event which even Lou Brock in an interview with New York sportswriter Red Foley, couldn't remember ever having accomplished—one thinks of Ty Cobb, who established homesteading rights to home plate with 35 steals of home, the most in history. One can almost envision Cobb, his somewhat cruel gray eyes now mischievously bright with contempt for the pitcher, jockeying for position off third, deliciously contemplating his next move. One can see his eyes fire, and in the next nanosecond so too would Cobb, racing down the base path, his movements positively purring with his every step. Sometimes he would pull up short, hoping to get trapped in a run down and either moving up his fellow base runners—part of his baserunning philosophy, "If you keep them throwing the ball long enough, somebody is sure to throw it away"—or breaking for home where, with spikes held high, he would come barreling into the catcher. Cobb was successful more times than not in his brazen attempt to alter the course of the game with tactical maneuvers that would have brought tears of joy to the eyes of Robert E. Lee.

But while Cobb is the prototypical example of the player who stole home, he came up far short of the requisite 400 homers to qualify for inclusion in this trivia question. One must look elsewhere to the most unlikely of places: to Babe Ruth. Those whose memories are plucked from prevailing winds only remember Ruth as an overweight outfielder whose movements were lumbered with the baggage of age. But in his youth, Ruth moved with a fluidity and grace that has not become part of his legend. Throughout his career Ruth stole 123 bases, including four in World Series play—the same number as Cobb—and 10 times stole home.

The only other player with 400 or more homers and 10 or more stolen bases was Lou Gehrig, who hit 493 home runs in his major league career and stole home no less than 15 times out of his 102 total steals—all at the front ends of double steals. Gehrig had the highest career percentage of stealing home of any player with 10 or more. The highest percentage for a player stealing home in one year belongs to Cleveland's Vic Power, who stole home twice in one game against the Detroit Tigers on August 14, 1958, tying the single–game record. That year saw him steal only one other base all season.

WHO WAS THE OLDEST PLAYER EVER TO APPEAR IN A MAJOR LEAGUE GAME?

Baseball not only builds character, it builds characters as well. And no character was bigger than Leroy "Satchel" Paige who, depending upon what writer was interviewing him, would give a different birthdate. All the better to add to the legend—and the mysterious aura surrounding him. It is therefore possible to read that Satchel Paige was born on September 18, 1899, September 11, 1904, July 25, 1905, July 7, 1906, July 18, 1908, August 27, 1908, September 18, 1908, September 22, 1908 or July 22, 1909—depending upon the reference source used. And "Satch" himself? When asked how old he was, he once just howled and said, "How old would you be if you didn't know how old you were?" But because his date is "officially"—whatever the hell that means—recorded as July 7, 1906, he is accorded the "honor" of being the oldest "rookie" ever to break into the major leagues at the age of 42 in 1948.

But baseball's Methuselah would go on . . . and on . . . and on. . . . He became the oldest ever to appear in an All–Star game at the age of 57, the oldest to appear in a major league game at age 59 plus change when he made his last major league appearance for the Kansas City A's in 1965. This was a three–inning stint that saw Satchel and his "hesitation" pitch strike out one and allow only one hit, and then go on to become the oldest ever to appear in a game in organized ball, when, in 1966, he made a brief appearance for the Peninsula Club in the Carolina League. Paige also became the oldest man ever to come to bat in a major league game when, in his one game as a Kansas City A, he struck out, thus eclipsing the geriatric record held by Nick Altrock. Both Paige and Altrock thus top the old–timer records held by George Blanda and Archie Moore in other sports. The records for performances by oldest players in each category follow:

PERFORMANCES BY OLDEST PLAYERS

PERFORMANCE BY PLAYER	AGE (Year/Month)	TEAM	DATE
Pitched, Satchel Paige	59–2	Kansas City A's	9/25/65
Batted (0-1), Satchel Paige	59–2	Kansas City A's	9/25/65
Caught, Jim O'Rourke	52–1	New York Giants	9/20/04
Base hit, Minnie Minoso	53–9	Chicago White Sox	9/12/76
Double, Jack Quinn	47–11	Brooklyn Dodgers	6/7/32
Triple, Nick Altrock	48–0	Washington Senators	9/30/24
Homer, Jack Quinn	45–11	Philadelphia A's	6/7/30
Grand Slam Homer, Tony Perez	42–11	Cincinnati Reds	5/13/85
Run Scored, Charlie O'Leary	52–11	St. Louis Browns	9/30/34
RBI, Jack Quinn	47–11	Brooklyn Dodgers	6/7/32
Stolen base, Arlie Latham	50–5	New York Giants	8/18/09
Played 100 games, Cap Anson	45	Chicago Cubs	1897
Won Game (relief), Jack Quinn	48–1	Brooklyn Dodgers	8/14/32
Lost Game (relief), Hoyt Wilhelm	48–11	Los Angeles Dodgers	6/24/72
Pitched CG (won), Phil Niekro	46–5	New York Yankees	10/6/85
Shutout, Phil Niekro	46–6	New York Yankees	10/6/85
No–hitter, Cy Young	41–3	Boston Red Sox	6/30/08

WHO IS THE ONLY PLAYER TO BE NAMED ROOKIE OF THE YEAR, MOST VALUABLE PLAYER, AND CY YOUNG AWARD WINNER?

The Cy Young Award, last of baseball's three great awards, was first presented by the Baseball Writers back in 1956. Originally conceived as an award to the outstanding pitcher, it was later to be subdivided into two awards, one for each league in 1958. But for the moment, and the season as well, the first winner of the award was Don Newcombe, recognized for his outstanding 27–7 season and league–leading won–lost percentage of .794. "Newk" also coupled the Cy Young Award that year with the winning of the National League's Most Valuable Player Award for his part in leading his team, the Brooklyn Dodgers, to the pennant. And could add both to his overflowing trophy case already bedecked with the very first National League Rookie of the Year Award given to him in 1949, the only man ever to win all three major awards. Tom Seaver is the only other pitcher who has ever won the Rookie of the Year honor and gone on to win the Cy Young Award, but Seaver was never accorded MVP honors. And Sandy Koufax, Vida Blue, Denny McLain, and Bob Gibson have all won the MVP and Cy Young awards, but none has ever been named Rookie of the Year.

WHAT PLAYER BOTH ENDED AND STARTED THE LONGEST TWO PLAYING STREAKS IN MAJOR LEAGUE HISTORY?

The determination to play every day, day in and day out, for years on end, takes something more than a conscious will, it takes perseverance, good fortune, and an understanding manager. The first player to be blessed with all three was Everett Scott, who played very well indeed at short for almost nine consecutive years. Starting his streak with the Boston Red Sox on

June 20, 1916, and continuing with the Yankees after Jake Ruppert shook the plum tree in Boston and brought him to New York during the 1921 off-season, along with Sad Sam Jones and Bullet Joe Bush, for their old shortstop Roger Peckinpaugh and a handful of silver. During Scott's streak he set an all–time major league record for most years—leading shortstops in fielding average eight consecutive seasons, and leading shortstops in put outs, assists, and double plays. Finally, as it must to all things, Scott's streak came to an end on May 5, 1925, after 1,307 consecutive games, when Pee Wee Wanninger was sent in to play shortstop for him.

It was that same Wanninger who would, less than a month later, start another consecutive–game streak, this one the all–time record. For on June 1 of that very same year, the weak–hitting Wanninger was called back to the bench by Yankee manager Miller Huggins who replaced him with a pinch hitter named Lou Gehrig. The following day first baseman Wally Pipp went to Huggins and said, "I don't feel equal to getting back in there," still not over a headache that had benched him the day before. That would be, in the words of Pipp, "The two most expensive aspirins in history," as Gehrig took his place at first and didn't sit down until 2,130 games later. And it had all started with Pee Wee Wanninger, who had been bookended by the two greatest consecutive–game streaks in history.

NAME THE ONLY PLAYER TO PLAY BEHIND THE WINNING "PERFECT" PITCHER IN TWO PERFECT GAMES.

The Perfect Game is baseball's version of Halley's Comet—pronounced as in O'Malley, as is everything else in baseball—its occurrence about as rare. Since the first sighting of a Perfect Game back in 1880, there have been just 13 thrown in Major League history—or a "Barker's Dozen" if you discount Len Barker's, as one wag did, commenting, "How can anything be 'Perfect' in Cleveland?"

And yet, while there have been so few Perfect Games they could almost be counted on one's fingers or fingers and toes, if pushed—there have been more than a handful of players who have played in more than one. The first three of this exclusive group played in both Cy Young's Perfect game of 1904 and Addie Joss' 1908 Classic: Patsy Dougherty and Fred Parent, both of whom played behind Young on the winning side for the Red Sox and on the losing side for the White Sox against Joss, and Ossee Schreckengost, who played on the losing side in both, the Joss game his last Major League game ever. The fourth of this small group was Junior Gilliam, who played on the losing side in Don Larsen's Perfect Game in '56 and on the winning side in Sandy Koufax's 27-men-up-27-men-down game in 1965. Then there is Wes Covington, who played on two winning sides, albeit not behind the winning "Perfect" pitcher each time. Covington was a member of the Milwaukee Braves on May 26, 1959, the night that Harvey Haddix threw his 12-inning "Perfect" game, only to lose to the Braves and Lew Burdette in the 13th. Covington also played behind the winning "Perfect" pitcher on June 21, 1964 when Jim Bunning threw the first Perfect Perfect Game in modern National League history. But it was the sixth member of this two-timer group, one Reginald Martinez Jackson, who accomplished the unique feat of playing behind the winning "Perfect" pitcher in two Perfect Games when on May 8, 1968, "Reggie" played behind Catfish Hunter as a member of the Oakland A's and on September 30, 1984, he played behind Mike Witt as a member of the California Angels.

WHO WAS THE ONLY PLAYER IN UNIFORM AT ALL THREE 19–STRIKEOUT GAMES IN MODERN HISTORY?

There have been spearcarriers to the greatness of others through baseball's long and illustrious history: Tracy Stallard, who threw Roger Maris his 61st home run; Tom Zachary, who threw Ruth his 60th; Don Liddle, who threw the pitch Vic Wertz hit to deep center field that Willie Mays caught in the 1954 World Series; Joe Krakauskas, who gave up Joe DiMaggio's final hit in his 56–game hitting streak; Jack Fisher, who threw Ted Williams his 521st and last home run; Willie Mitchell, the losing pitcher in Babe Ruth's first major league win; Chick Fullis, who replaced Joe Medwick in left field in the seventh game of the 1934 Series when Medwick was "asked to leave" by Commissioner Landis; shortstop Harry Lunte, who took the striken Ray Chapman's position after Chapman was beaned by Carl Mays on August 16, 1920; Willie Mays, himself, who was in the batter's box when Bobby Thomson hit his home run in 1951; and Dick Stuart, who was in the batter's box when Bill Mazeroski hit his in 1960, etc., etc., ad nauseum.

And then there have been the stars, the top bananas, who have been the participants—a list that would make the New York telephone directory look small by comparison. But it is rare for a player to both have had a starring role and a bit part in the making of history, especially history that involved the same achievement. However, that is exactly what happened when, as a member of the New York Mets, Nolan Ryan witnessed first Steve Carlton's 19-strikeout performance against the Mets, September 15, 1969, then Tom Seaver's 19–strikeout game for the Mets against the San Diego Padres the following April 22, and followed that up by pitching his own 19–strikeout game while a member of the California Angels, August 12, 1974, thereby making Ryan the only player in uniform at all three modern–day 19–K games.

WHAT TWO PLAYING BROTHERS' TOTAL MAJOR LEAGUE CAREER SPANNED THE MOST YEARS?

One of the longest–running brother acts in American politics was the Clintons, older brother George who served as vice president of the United States under two presidents, Thomas Jefferson and James Madison, and his younger brother, DeWitt, who served as governor of New York and is credited with sponsoring the Erie Canal. Together these two brothers, separated in age by 30 years, were governors of New York from 1777 to 1828. Baseball's answer to the Clinton brothers are the Fowler brothers, Art and Jesse. Separated in age by 24 years, their Major League careers spanned 40 long years. Jesse put in one year as a pitcher with the 1924 St. Louis Cardinals and his (much) younger brother, Art, pitched for the Cincinnati Reds, Los Angeles Angels, and Los Angeles Dodgers from 1954 through 1964.

WHAT BROTHERS FINISHED THEIR CAREERS WITH THE SAME EXACT BATTING AVERAGE?

When George and Harry Wright took the field for the Boston Red Stockings back in 1871, they formed what would be the first set of playing brothers. It was an act that would set well, and be repeated many times in baseball history from that date forth. Sometimes the gathering began to take on the look of a family picnic or an original snapshot of the Flying Wallandas, as when the entire Anson family formed a team for Marshalltown, Ia. or when the five Delehanty and five O'Neill brothers all made it to the big leagues. And other times it would provide comparisons, statistics, and even trivia questions, almost baseball's version of the kaleidoscope, as the brothers performed in different patterns with constantly changing sets of designs. It was thus possible to find the following association of brothers: The first two brothers to appear as battery mates are the Whites, Deacon and Will, in the National League, and the O'Neills, Mike and Jack, in the American; the first brothers to face each other on the mound, the Barnes, Jesse and Virgil; the first brothers to play against each other in a World Series, the Johnstons, Doc and Jimmy, in the 1920 World Series; the first brothers to each win batting titles, the Walkers, Dixie and Harry; the first, and only, all–brother outfield, the Alous, Matty, Jesus, and Felipe, on September 15, 1963; and the first brothers to play against each other in a League Championship Series, the Iorgs, Dane and Garth, in the 1985 American League Series.

But while brothers reflect each other, rarely do they mirror one another's performance. The Meusel brothers, Bob and Irish, came close to mirroring each other, finishing with .309 and .310 averages after 11 years each in the majors. However, it remained for the Johnson brothers, Bob and Roy, two–part Cherokees who were both batsmen, to become the spitting image of each other, at least where batting averages were concerned. Each hit .296 during their total of 23 years in the majors—"Indian" Bob playing 13 years for the Philadelphia A's, Washington Senators, and Boston Red Sox from 1933 through 1945 and older brother Roy playing 10 years for the Detroit Tigers, Boston Red Sox, New York Yankees, and Boston Braves from 1929 through 1938.

And for those who believe that baseball is truly a family game, there is a father–son act that rivals that of the Johnsons, over on the pitching side of the ledger. Both the Monteagudos, father Rene and son Aurielo, had the exact same record for their major league careers, three wins and seven losses.

WHAT PITCHER AND CATCHER WERE BATTERYMATES FOR THE LONGEST PERIOD OF TIME?

Tim McCarver, who spent the better part of eight seasons catching the left–handed offerings of Steve Carlton for both the Cards and the Phillies, tried to put the special relationship existing between a pitcher and a catcher in perspective, "When Steve and I die, we're going to be buried in the same cemetery, 60 feet, six inches apart." However, McCarver and Carlton were not the first batterymates to be reunited on a second team for an extended period of time. Grover Cleveland Alexander and his favorite catcher, Bill Killefer, were traded in tandem from the Phillies to the Cubs in 1917, there to continue as an "item" for a total of 11 years. And Cy Young and his catcher, Lou Criger, put in three different terms of service together with three different teams, Cleveland and St. Louis of the National League before the turn of the century and from 1901 through 1908, the Boston Pilgrims–cum–Red Sox in the American League, spending a total of 13 lucky years only 60 feet, six inches apart. But it wasn't merely a question of those who get traded together staying together. Hall of Fame pitcher Ed Walsh and catcher Billy Sullivan spent 11 years together on the Chicago White Sox, from 1904 through 1914—being so much the company men that their sons, Ed Walsh and Billy Sullivan, were batterymates together for the ChiSox in 1932, the only pair of father–son batterymates. Other pitching–catching combinations who spent their entire careers together on the same team include Whitey Ford and Yogi Berra, who worked together for 12 years during the 1950s and on into the early 1960s, and Mickey Lolich and Bill Freehan, who played together on the Detroit Tigers for 13 years during the 1960s and on into the 1970s. But the longevity award for longest-running batterymates in a major league career belongs to the combination of Red Ruffing and Bill Dickey, whose joint careers with the New York Yankees extend over 14 years, from mid–1930 through 1942 and for one more year, 1946, following the return of the two veterans from World War II.

NAME THE LAST LEFT–HANDED CATCHER IN THE MAJORS.

If, as Heywood Hale Broun said, "Being left–handed is a state of mind," then 11 major league lefties must have thought of themselves as right–handed as they took up their stations behind the bat as catchers. Back in that time known as, "the good old days"—today being "the good old days" of tomorrow—being left–handed was hardly a disqualifying factor for playing any position on the diamond. Both Fred Tenney and Babe Ruth started as left–handed catchers, Ruth catching at St. Mary's Industrial School in Baltimore, where the only catcher's mitt available was right–handed, forcing Ruth to flip it off every time he threw the ball, an early–day version of Pete Gray.

The very first major leaguer to catch left–handed was Fergy Malone, who started with the 1871 Philadelphia Athletics of the National Association and continued for 172 games of his 218–game career from 1871 through 1884. The other six who caught left–handed before the turn of the century were Cal Broughton, who caught 35 games for six teams between 1883 and 1888; Phil Baker, who caught 62 games from 1883 through 1886; John Humphries, who caught 75 games in 1883 and 1884; Pop Tate, who caught 202 games from 1885 through 1890; and the premier left–handed catcher of all time, Jack Clements, who caught 1,073 games—more than Hall of Famer Roger Bresnahan—primarily for the Philadelphia Phillies, 1884 to 1900. Those who caught left–handed in the majors after the cusp of the century were Joe Wall, who caught seven games for the Giants and Dodgers in 1901 and 1902; Tom Doran, who caught 46 games for the Red Sox and Tigers from 1904 through 1906; of more recent vintage, Dale Long, who was impressed into duty for two games by the 1958 Chicago Cubs; and, the most recent one, Mike Squires of the Chicago White Sox, normally a left–handed first baseman, but for two days in 1980 a catcher, making his last appearance on May 7, 1980 as the last left–handed catcher in major league history.

But Squires, not content to rest on one oar, also makes history of yet another sort: he is also the last left–handed third baseman in baseball history, playing 14 games in 1983 and 1984. Unless, of course, one is to believe the *MacMillan Baseball Encyclopedia* which lists Wade Boggs as a third baseman who "bats right, throws left."

WHO WAS THE LAST SWITCH–HITTER TO WIN THE MOST VALUABLE PLAYER AWARD IN THE AMERICAN LEAGUE?

The only excuse for including this old chestnut is to prove that some of those thought–drops at the scrivener's favorite watering holes do not escape his attention. And it is devoutly to be wished that the reader can excuse him, like Jack The Ripper, on the grounds that it is human nature. Nothing more. For the answer is Vida Blue, who won the Most Valuable Player award back in 1971 and was a switch–hitter. No kidding! You can, as Casey Stengel said, "Look it up." Switch-hitter Pete Rose was the National League Most Valuable Player some two years later, rendering this question one–dimensional. At best!

WHAT SON OF A FAMOUS MAJOR LEAGUE PITCHER BROKE UP JOE DIMAGGIO'S LONGEST CONSECUTIVE GAME HITTING STREAK?

On the night of July 17, 1941 Joe DiMaggio went to bat four times in a vain attempt to preserve his 56–game hitting streak, a contract from Heinz 57 already in his back pocket, ready for the signing. DiMaggio faced Cleveland's starting pitcher, Al Smith, three times and hit two sizzling drives down the third–base line somewhere in the direction of Ken Keltner, only to be robbed by his teammate of just nine days earlier on the American League All–Star team when both had scored in the ninth inning to beat the National League. Yet on this night Keltner was having no part of teaming with DiMaggio again and converted both drives into spectacular outs. Sandwiched between Keltner's two fielding gems, DiMaggio had walked. In his fourth appearance that night, DiMag came up with the bases full and one out to face Cleveland relief pitcher Jim Bagby, Jr., whose father Jim Bagby, Sr., had pitched twenty years earlier, winning 31 games in 1920 for the same Indians. Bagby threw one ball and one strike and then got DiMaggio to smash directly at Cleveland shortstop Lou Boudreau who converted it into an inning–ending double play. DiMaggio would go on after that fateful night to hit in 17 additional consecutive games and, counting, the aforementioned All-Star game, would hit in 75 of 76 straight games. During that 56–game streak DiMaggio had 91 hits in 223 at bats for a .408 average. Incredibly, over the same period, May 15 through July 16, Ted Williams would hit .412.

However, this was *not* DiMaggio's longest consecutive hitting streak! In but his second year in professional baseball, the then 18–year–old DiMaggio, playing for the San Francisco Seals—where he, as future teammate Lefty Gomez would later taunt him, "Took away his older brother Vince's job"—hit in 61 consecutive games, amassing 104 hits in 257 official times at bat to set a Pacific Coast League record. On July 25, 1933, the young sensation faced Oakland pitcher Ed Walsh, son of Hall of Famer Ed Walsh. Walsh was to hold DiMaggio hitless in five times at bat.

But even DiMaggio's 61–game streak was not the longest in organized ball. That record belongs to one Joe Wilhoit of Wichita of the Western League who hit in 69 consecutive games back in 1919, a feat which earned him a promotion to the majors where he played for all of five games in the Boston Red Sox outfield next to Babe Ruth.

WHO APPEARED AS A PINCH HITTER IN HIS LAST MAJOR LEAGUE APPEARANCE IN THE SAME GAME IN WHICH BABE RUTH HIT HIS 60TH HOME RUN?

New York has always been a place where reputations are built taller than buildings. And none had a bigger reputation than Babe Ruth, who, in a field devoted to fashioning halos for performers, wore a special nimbus. And so, on the afternoon of September 30, 1927, 10,000 lovers of the arts thronged out to pay homage to Ruth, and to see history in the making, as he continued his assault on the all–time home run record, one he had set himself just six years before. Paul Gallico, writing about that moment before it actually occurred, said, "Once he had that 59, that number 60 was as sure as the setting sun. A more determined athlete than George Herman Ruth never lived. He is one of the few utterly dependable news stories in sports." So just as the sun started setting in the eighth inning, Ruth came up to face Washington pitcher Tom Zachary and parked one of Zachary's pitches in his favorite spot in the right field bleachers, giving him his 60th and the Yankees the game, then minced his way around the bases as the bellow of the throng paid tribute to him. Few of those who remained would notice that history of another sort was being made the next inning when Washington sent up a pinch hitter for Zachary, the great Walter Johnson, making his last Major League appearance. Johnson had been used as pinch hitter several times during his long 21–year career, coming to bat in that capacity 110 times and connecting safely 21 of those. Over the course of his career, Johnson had had a total of 549 hits—including 42 in 1925 when he hit .433, the highest for any pitcher with over 90 at bats—and finished his career as one of the only five men in history, along with Cy Young Joe Wood, Red Ruffing, and Happy Jack Stivetts, to have over 100 wins and 500 hits.

And the last game for another pitching great came in yet another historic game—the game in which Ted Williams became the sixth and last, American Leaguer to hit .400 in a season. Batting .39955 going into the last day's double-header against the Philadelphia A's, Williams asked Red Sox manager Joe Cronin for permission to play rather than sit out the twin bill and get a free pass into the .400 magic circle on a rounding-off technicality. In the first game Teddy Ballgame went four-for-five. And in the second added a two-for-three effort to cement his claim as a legitimate .400 hitter. It was in that last game that a 41-year-old left-hander named Lefty Grove made his last Major League appearance. Claiming "I'm throwing just as hard as I ever did, only the ball's just not getting there as fast," Grove lost a 7-1 decision to A's pitcher Fred Caligiuri, the last game Caligiuri ever won in the Majors.

Baseball's everlasting continuity—that same continuity that had Babe Ruth playing his last game within 24 hours of the first night game in Major League history—was best illustrated by a game on May 2, 1939, the day Lou Gehrig benched himself and ended his 2,130-game endurance record. For on that day the Detroit Tigers unveiled a young 19-year-old pitcher they had just purchased from Seattle for 50,000 hard-to-come-by Depression dollars: Freddie Hutchinson. Unfortunately, in his first Major League appearance, young "hutch" looked like an accident on its way to happening as he locked bumpers with a Murderer's Row of sluggers hell-bent on denting the ball. And Hutchinson as well. Batting against the young reliever, the Gehrig-less Yankees got six runs on four hits and five walks in just ⅔ of an inning on their way to a 22-2 win.

WHAT CATCHER CAUGHT THE MOST NO-HITTERS?

The phrase, "tools of ignorance," used to describe the catcher's protective equipment is a contradiction in terms. For the catcher is the team's quarterback, the player who not only calls every pitch, but every alignment. How else can you explain that some of the most successful managers in baseball history were catchers? One of those who called every pitch in four no–hitters was Ray Schalk, the Hall of Fame catcher for the Chicago White Sox for 17 years, during which he caught no fewer than four no–hitters—James Scott's in 1914, Joe Benz's in 1914, Eddie Cicotte's in 1917, and Charlie Robertson's perfect game in 1922—an all–time record.

Ten other backstops have been on the receiving end of baseball history three times: Lou Criger (1904, 1908, and 1910); Bill Carrigan (1911, 1916, and 1916); Val Pininich (1916, 1920, and 1923); Luke Sewell (1931, 1935, and 1937); Jim Hegan (1947, 1948, and 1951); Yogi Berra (1951, 1951, and 1956); Del Crandall (1954, 1960, and 1960); Johnny Edwards (1965, 1965, and 1968); and Jeff Torborg, the only man, besides Gus Triandos, to catch no–hitters in both leagues (1965, 1970, and 1973).

Pininich is the only catcher to catch no–hitters with three different teams (Joe Bush's for the A's in 1916, Walter Johnson's for the Senators in 1920, and Howard Ehmke's for the Red Sox in 1923), mirroring two of the most unusual no–hit receiving pieces of trivia: three catchers, each one with a last name beginning with the letter "H," handled Bob Feller's three no–hitters: Hemsley, Hayes, and Hegan. And both Luke Sewell and Del Crandall caught all three of theirs against the same team—Sewell against the Browns and Crandall against the Phillies.

WHAT PLAYER WENT 3–FOR–3 IN HIS ONLY GAME IN THE MAJORS?

Those non-pitchers who have managed to spend one game and one cup of coffee, of the instant variety, in the majors total no less than 349, according to the *MacMillan Baseball Encyclopedia*, where their names are writ large even if their accomplishments were small. Many in this veritable smorgasbord of one–day wonders have names that strike a small resonant note. Consider names like Eddie Gaedel or Walter Alston—who struck out in his only appearance, playing first in place of Cardinal first baseman Johnny Mize, who had been excused by the umpire the previous inning during an altercation—or Joe Evers, Johnny's brother, or even Charlie Lindstrom, Hall of Famer Freddie's son. Lindstrom, in fact, is noteworthy, not only because he got a hit in his only game—something that only 71 others accomplished—but his one hit in his one at-bat was a triple, giving him a batting average of 1.000 and a slugging average of 3.000; the highest ever for a major leaguer.

But perhaps the greatest day of one–dayers was on May 18, 1912 when the Detroit Tigers fielded a rag–tag team that looked like they had just emptied the mission. The game was known as the day of the Detroit Tiger walkout, a sympathy strike to protest Ty Cobb's suspension after he had gone into the stands to subdue a heckler in New York during the previous series. Cobb, whose temper was such that he could branch out and start franchises, had crossed that frontier from field to stand to retaliate against someone who had been riding him, and riding him hard, for years. The fan, one Claude Leuker, was a secretary to Tom Foley, the former sheriff, and had, in his infinite nonwisdom, "been picking on me for years," according to Cobb. Leuker finally learned physically that anything that riled the walking volcano was a mistake, as Cobb executed a two–step on his head. The private police in Highland Park refused to arrest Cobb, instead apprehending the fan. But umpire Silk O'Loughlin threw Cobb out of the game and American League president Ban Johnson, who had been in the stands, suspended the fiery Tiger. The entire Detroit team sent a telegram to Johnson demanding that Cobb be reinstated and threatening that they would not play their scheduled game in Philadelphia. Johnson, never a man to give in to threat, refused to lift the suspension. The Detroit team walked off the field.

Tiger Manager Hughie Jennings, to protect his franchise, desperately sent out a distress signal to the Philadelphia sandlots and to nearby St. Joseph's College calling for all players, paying them $50 and giving them a chance to be major leaguers, at least for the day. But putting this group of semi–pros in Tiger uniforms did not produce major leaguers any more than baking kittens in the oven produces biscuits. This group of miscasts, who could have had their pictures sent to the local constabulary for identification, both during and after the game, managed, with the aid of the creaking manager, Jennings, and an equally ancient coach, Deacon McGuire, to lose by the score of 24–2 to the real athletes on the field, the Athletics. And eight of those who bobbed to the surface for that one afternoon were never seen again after their one day as major leaguers—Jennings and a third baseman named Billy Maharg, who would crop up again as a go–between in the 1919 Black Sox scandal, the only two who would ever play ball again, and then just one more game apiece. But if there was anything to remember about the game, it was that one of the players, Ed Irvin, in three times up, had two triples, thereby giving him the most total bases for any one–day player, six, a .667 batting average, and a 2.000 SA.

Two other players were one–day wonders, almost Roy Hobbs types, popping up and then disappearing without a trace. One was Ray Jansen, who, as a one–day Brown back in 1910, had four singles in five at–bats and was never heard from again. The other was John Paciorek, brother of Tom Paciorek, who, on September 29, 1963, as a member of the Houston Colt .45s, went to the plate five times, walked twice, had three singles, and scored four runs, the only man in baseball history ever to go 3–for–3 in his only game.

WHO IS THE ONLY MAN TO PARTICIPATE IN TWO UNASSISTED TRIPLE PLAYS?

Arguably the most improbable of all events in the annals of baseball is the unassisted triple play, a play so rare that it has only been seen eight times in recorded major league history—seven times in regular season play and once in the World Series.

The very first time an unassisted triple play saw the light of day came on the afternoon of July 19, 1909, when, in the top of the second, Cleveland shortstop, Neal Ball, speared a liner off the bat of Boston's Amby McConnell, came directly down on second to double up Heinie Wagner, and then tagged out base runner Jake Stahl to complete his then one–of–a–kind accomplishment. Over the next 60 years, seven other players have turned the trick, including Bill Wambsganss in the fifth game of the 1920 World Series, the only second baseman to do so. But of all the men to be involved in triple plays, fielders, batters, and base runners—including four Hall of Famers: Bottomley, Hornsby, and the Waners—only one man has ever participated in two of these eight baseball originals: Jim Cooney, once as the perpetrator and another time as one of the three perpetratees. On May 7, 1925, Cooney was one of the three Cardinals retired by Pittsburgh shortstop Glenn Wright, and two years later, as a member of the Chicago Cubs, Cooney himself executed an unassisted triple play—the only man to participate in two unassisted triple plays and also to be involved with all four of the Hall of Famers caught with their bases down in those unassisted triple plays.

UNASSISTED TRIPLE PLAYS

PLAYER EXECUTING	POSITION	TEAM	DATE	INNING	BATTER, TEAM
Neal Ball	SS	Cleveland, AL	July 19, 1909	2nd	Amby McConnell, Boston
	Ball speared McConnell's line drive, came down on second to double up Heinie Wagner and tagged out Jake Stahl coming from first.				
Bill Wambsganss	2B	Cleveland, AL	October 10, 1920	5th	Clarence Mitchell, Brooklyn
	"Wamby" caught Clarence Mitchell's liner, stepped on second to retire Pete Kilduff and wheeled around to tag Otto Miller coming down from first.				
George Burns	1B	Boston, AL	September 14, 1923	2nd	Frank Brower, Cleveland
	Burns took Brower's line drive, reached out and tagged Walter Lutzke, who had been on first base, and then rushed down to second to tag base before base runner Joe Stephenson could return.				
Ernie Padgett	SS	Boston, NL	October 6, 1923	4th	Walter Holke, Philadelphia

PLAYER EXECUTING	POSITION	TEAM	DATE	INNING	BATTER, TEAM
	Padget took Holke's line drive, tagged second to retire Cotton Tierney, and then tagged out Cliff Lee who was coming into second.				
Glenn Wright	SS	Pittsburgh, NL	May 7, 1925	9th	Jim Bottomley, St. Louis
	Wright snared Bottomley's liner, touched second to retire Jim Cooney, and then tagged out Rogers Hornsby on his way into second.				
Jim Cooney	SS	Chicago, NL	May 30, 1927	4th	Paul Waner, Pittsburgh
	Cooney grabbed Waner's line drive, doubled Lloyd Waner off second, and then tagged out Clyde Barnhart, coming down from first.				
Johnny Neun	1B	Detroit, AL	May 31, 1927	9th	Homer Summa, Cleveland
	Neun snared Summa's liner and tagged first to double up Charlie Jamieson, then raced down toward second to tag out base runner Glenn Myatt before he could return to second, ending the game.				
Ron Hansen	SS	Washington, AL	July 29, 1968	1st	Joe Azcue, Cleveland
	Azcue's liner grabbed by Hansen who stepped on second, doubling up Dave Nelson and then tagged out Russ Snyder, barreling down from first.				

2nd Inning
The Batters

WHAT PLAYER HAD THE MOST MAJOR LEAGUE AT–BATS WITHOUT A HIT?

Dean Chance, a pitcher whose batting ability rivaled the acting ability of Pia Zadora, was once heard to lament, "I wish I were still playing; the designated hitter rule was made for me." Proponents for the designated hitter rule always make their case by invoking the name of Chance or Fred Gladding, the former Detroit and Houston pitcher, who went 1–for–63 during his 13–year career. But on the afternoon of July 30, 1969, Gladding had an answer for them with a base hit and a statement for the baseball world in general: "Now word will get around that I have a hot bat." But hot bat or no, Fred Gladding was not the worst hitting pitcher of all time. For those whose sensitivity comes out like hair on a comb, one must bring up the sorry plight of one Daryl Patterson, who, while pitching for Detroit and Pittsburgh between 1968 and 1974, went 0–for–35. Still, Patterson has to take a back seat to Randy Tate, who, in one year on the New York Mets' 1975 pitching staff, went 0–for–41. Restated, that's 0–for–the–season, the most at–bats without even matching Gladding's hot bat.

WHAT PLAYER HAD TO WAIT THE MOST YEARS BETWEEN BASE HITS?

When Minnie Minoso took his position in the batter's box as the designated hitter for the Chicago White Sox on September 11, 1976, he was coming to the plate for the first time in 12 years, his last appearance, also as a White Sox, dating back to 1964. But even though Minoso didn't get a hit that day, he did in one of his next two games, making it an even dozen years between base hits for Minoso. However, Minoso doesn't even come close to the record for the longest time between base hits, trailing two other elder statesman of baseball who came back after a long hiatus. One was Gabby Street, then manager of the St. Louis Cardinals, who inserted himself into the lineup as the catcher in a 1931 game. In Street's one appearance at the plate he singled, his first hit since 1912, 19 years before, but still two years shy of the record. For in 1934, St. Louis Browns coach Charley O'Leary, who had last played for the Cardinals in 1913, persuaded manager Rogers Hornsby to let him hit. And hit he did, getting a single 21 years after his previous major league hit, earning the record wait between drinks at the hit fountain.

NAME THE ONLY PLAYERS TO PLAY FOR 20 OR MORE YEARS WITHOUT EVER HITTING A HOMER.

To some players the future tense of the home run is the home run trot, a natural extension of the homer. For many the prototype of that trot was Babe Ruth who used to mince his way around the basepaths, making sure he adhered to the only suuperstition he ever admitted to: "Touching all four bases." But for others, the home run trot is unnatural, at best, somewhat like playing the violin in public and having to learn the instrument as one goes along; an acquired trait. One of those was Ozzie Smith, hardly one of baseball's greatest home run hitters, especially left-handed. After hitting one of his rarer-than-rare homers, Smith came to the realization, "I wanted to go into my home run trot, and then discovered that I didn't have one." Others have discovered that they too could never second the emotion of a home run trot, including three pitchers who played for over 20 years without ever having the need to perfect one: Waite Hoyt, who played 21 years from 1918 trough 1938, coming to bat 1284 times without a homer or a trot; Dutch Leonard, who played 20 years from 1933 through '53, coming to bat 1054 times without the need for such a trot; and Don Sutton, who has played 20 years, from 1965 through '85, and has come to bat 1331 times without ever having hit a homer or going into the requisite trot. One other man, Hoyt Wilhelm, gets an honorable mention. For Wilhelm played for 20 consecutive years without going into a trot, albeit the *last* 20 years of his career. He did have one chance to practice his trot, his very first time up in the majors. But is was something he would never have a chance to do again as he joins the other three—20 years without a trot, even if they were the last 20 of his career.

WHO WAS THE ONLY PLAYER IN MAJOR LEAGUE HISTORY TO HIT A HOME RUN IN HIS FIRST TIME AT BAT AND A HOME RUN IN HIS LAST TIME AT BAT?

Fifty players have hit home runs in their first at-bats in the Majors, including eleven who would never hit another during their careers—Dan Bankhead, Hoyt Wilhelm, Bill LeFebvre, Don Rose and Andre David amongst them. But only one, John Miller, would also hit in a home run in his last time at bat in the big leagues. Miller, who was the only New York Yankee ever to hit a home run his first time at bat, September 11, 1966, also hit one his last time at bat, September 23, 1969, for the Los Angeles Dodgers—thus becoming the only man other than Ted Williams to hit a homer in his last Major League at-bat. Ironically, they would be his only two home runs in 61 times at bat.

One other player deserves inclusion with the Wilhelms, Bankheads, LeFebvres, Roses Davids and Millers: Ron Allen. Allen, Richie's brother, played for the St. Louis Cardinals in 1972, coming to bat eleven times and getting but one hit, that a home run, making him the only man in Major League history whose every hit in his career was a home run.

WHO IS THE ONLY PLAYER TO LEAD THE LEAGUE IN MOST HOME RUNS AND LEAST STRIKEOUTS IN THE SAME YEAR?

Former home–run hitter Ralph Kiner is generally credited with the line, "Home runs are down at the end of the bat." Ralph should know of what he speaks because home–run hitters, by the very nature of their from–the–end–of–the–bat—not to mention from–the-heels, swing, strike out frequently. And Kiner was one of those who struck out frequently, more frequently than he hit home runs. In fact, every player who has hit 50 or more home runs has struck out more times than hit homers. One exception is Johnny Mize who hit 51 homers to tie the aforementioned Mr. Kiner in 1947 for the league lead, but struck out only 42 times to Kiner's 81. Two other home–run leaders, Lou Gehrig in 1934 and 1936 and Ted Kluszewski in 1955, also struck out fewer times than they connected for homers: Gehrig hitting 49 homers in both years and striking out only 31 times in 1934 and 46 in 1936 and Klu also smiting 49 homers in 1954 and striking out only 35 times. But the all–time leader in home runs–to–strikeout ratio is Tommy Holmes who led the National League with 28 homers in 1945 and struck out only nine times, tops in the major leagues that year.

WHAT PLAYER HIT THE MOST HOME RUNS WITHOUT EVER HITTING A GRAND SLAMMER?

Someone once asked Garry Maddox to describe his first major league grand slam. Maddox thought for a moment and then replied, "Well, as I remember it, the bases were loaded . . . ." Lou Gehrig could remember a record 23 times the bases were loaded out of the 493 homers he hit during his career, usually with the likes of Babe Ruth, Earl Combs, and others in the Yankees' deadly "Murderer's Row" who preceded him in the lineup. On the other side of the bat, Willie Kirkland, who played for the San Francisco Giants, Cleveland Indians, Baltimore Orioles, and Washington Senators during a nine–year career, couldn't remember once when the bases were loaded, having hit none out of his 148 career home runs—a record of sorts.

WHAT LEAGUE HOME-RUN CHAMPION NEVER HIT ANOTHER AFTER LEADING HIS LEAGUE?

Back in the days when men were men and women were damned glad of it, the home run was the ghetto area of baseball. Base running derring–do was the basic offensive weapon, courtesy of the old Baltimore Orioles' winning philosophy adopted by every team, winner or no. The home run, in fact, was as glamorous as an unmade bed, and the baseball world responded, showing a profound contempt for the skills of home-run hitters. One of those who has become lost somewhere in the annals of time—and baseball as well—is Fred Odwell, who plied his trade for four years with the Cincinnati Reds back in the troglodyte age, 1904 to 1907. Odwell made one home run in his rookie year and then, in 1908, outdid not only himself but also the rest of the National League as he hit a league-leading nine. They would be his last nine even though he would go on to play for two more seasons, leaving him with a total of 10 home runs (then spelled as one word), the lowest lifetime total ever for a home-run leader. Since 1920, the year the Caesars of baseball implanted a rabbit's pulse in the baseball to accelerate their hoped–for new weapon—the home run—the lowest number of lifetime homers belongs to Tommy Holmes with 89, followed closely by Nick Etten with 88, but still nowhere near Mr. Odwell's 10. He was the only home-run champion never to hit another home run after attaining his Everest.

WHO WAS THE LAST PLAYER TO HIT MORE HOME RUNS THAN THE REST OF HIS TEAM, COMBINED?

Twelve times in baseball history one-man strong–arm squads have outhomered the rest of their team. The first time someone outstripped the rest of his teammates combined occurred back in the prehistoric days of 1902 when Philadelphia's Shad Barry hit three of the Phillies' five homers; the last time came in 1944 when Washington's Stan Spence hit 18 of the Senator's 33 total home runs. But outhomering the rest of one's team does not necessarily ensure the slugger that he has also outstripped the league as well, only five of the twelve one–man homer champs also hitting more than the rest of the league combined.

PLAYERS WHO HAVE OUT-HOMERED THEIR ENTIRE TEAM

NAME	CLUB	YEAR	TOTAL
S. Barry	Philadelphia, NL	1902	3 of team's 5
*J. Scheckard	Brooklyn, NL	1903	9 of team's 15
*H. Lumley	Brooklyn, NL	1904	9 of team's 15
D. Hoblitzell	Cincinnati, NL	1911	11 of team's 21
*B. Ruth	Boston, AL	1918	11 of team's 15
J. Wood	Cleveland, AL	1918	5 of team's 9
*B. Ruth	Boston, AL	1919	29 of team's 33
*C. Williams	Philadelphia, NL	1927	30 of team's 57
W. Berger	Boston, NL	1930	38 of team's 66
W. Berger	Boston, NL	1931	19 of team's 34
J. Foxx	Boston, AL	1938	50 of team's 98
S. Spence	Washington, AL	1944	18 of team's 33

*Also led League in home runs.

WHAT PLAYER HAD THE HIGHEST BATTING AVERAGE FOR HIS FIRST FULL YEAR IN THE MAJORS? FOR HIS LAST?

Fate has a fickle habit of bestowing its fame on those it later takes by the scruff of the neck and hurls overboard. One of those who ran afoul of fate in such a manner was Joe Jackson, better known as "Shoeless" Joe Jackson, the great Cleveland Indian and Chicago White Sox outfielder, who, unfortunately, was more associated with a third team than either of the two above-mentioned, the Chicago "Black Sox" of 1919. Jackson was a natural talent, one who could almost will a hit with his bat, leading three minor leagues in batting his first three years in organized baseball: the Carolina League in 1908 with a .346 average while playing for his hometown Greenville team, the South Atlantic League in 1909 with a .358 average, and the Southern Association in 1910 with a .354 average. But Jackson also possessed another natural talent, the talent of undoing himself, as he proved in the minors by three times stealing a base already occupied and in the majors by continually wandering away from the ballpark in search of something else which could better occupy his time. Called up twice during his first three years by Connie Mack, Jackson saw limited action with the Philadelphia A's before being farmed out, Mack tiring of trying to instill discipline that Jackson's head rejected. Finally, after two tryouts with the A's—and a total of 10 games in which he went 8–for–40—Mack had had enough and released his prodigal player. All Jackson ever wanted to do was own a farm, and now, taking Mack's advice to heart, he tried to bat his way back into the Majors. Cleveland took a chance on Jackson, bringing him back up to the Majors. After he had won his third straight minor league batting title for a 20-game stay in 1910. This time around Jackson showed some hints of his future greatness, batting .387 in 20 games. The following year, 1911, Jackson finally came into his own, and, in his first full year in the Majors, hit .408, the highest batting average for any Major Leaguer's first full year and the sixth highest in modern history. Unfortunately, that was the same year that Ty Cobb outdid him—both with his ways, batting .420, and with his wiles, refusing to shake hands with the friendly, slow–witted Jackson—thus causing Jackson to anguish through the last month of the season, wondering why the great Cobb "was slightin' me."

Jackson, whose first–year batting average was the highest ever, would go on to prove he was the turtle and not the mock with his performance over the next nine years, first with Cleveland and then with the Chicago White Sox, to whom he was traded in 1915. By 1920 he had become one of baseball's superstars. Unfortunately, that greatness had already been compromised. He had accepted money to alter the outcome of the 1919 World Series. Still, he batted .382 in 1920. But time was running out on "Shoeless Joe," who had already pawned his future for enough money to buy his farm. By the end of the 1920 season, the eight men who had mortgaged their futures were made to pay up and banned forever from organized baseball. Joe Jackson, who couldn't say, "It ain't so," was one of them. He left the game forever with not only the highest batting average for his first full year, the highest average for his last year, but a .356 lifetime average—the third highest in the history of baseball and the highest of anyone not enshrined in the Baseball Hall of Fame, a place that is also barred to him forever.

WHO IS THE ONLY AMERICAN LEAGUE BATTER TO WIN THE BATTING CHAMPIONSHIP WITHOUT HITING A HOME RUN?

From the day he first stepped on the diamond, Rod Carew has used his bat like a magic wand, putting the ball wherever he wanted, although rarely in the seats. Carew's magic worked for him seven times in all as he won the American League batting titles in 1969, 1972, 1973, 1974, 1975, 1977, and 1978 with averages that ranged from .318 to .388. But it was his second batting championship in 1972, when he hit but .318, that saw Carew win the batting crown without hitting a single home run amongst his 170 hits. Carew thus became the third—and only American Leaguer—ever to win a batting title without benefit of a home run. The previous two times this feat had been accomplished were in the National League in 1902, when Pittsburgh's Ginger Beaumont won with a .357 average and no homers, and in 1918, when Brooklyn's Zack Wheat won with a .335 average and, again, no home runs.

NAME THE THREE PLAYERS WHO HIT BOTH A HOME RUN AND A TRIPLE IN THEIR FIRST MAJOR LEAGUE GAME.

Hitting a home run in their first major league game—let alone their first at-bat in the majors—is enough to justify any ballplayer's election to the Trivia Hall of Fame. But hitting a home run and a triple in their very first game makes their trivia stock double in value, if not, to continue the metaphor, triple. Since the year Zip there have been only three men who have managed to accomplish this singular act: Hank "Bow Wow" Arft, in his first game for the St. Louis Browns on July 27, 1948; Lloyd Merriman of the Cincinnati Reds, on April 24, 1949; and Frank Ernaga, of the Chicago Cubs on May 24, 1957. Not content to rest on their trivia laurels, this threesome rode their particular hobbyhorses to the ends of their careers. Each winding up with an equal number of home runs and triples—Arft, 13 homers and 13 triples; Merriman, 12 homers and 12 triples; and Ernaga, two homers and two triples.

WHAT PLAYER FINISHED SECOND THE MOST TIMES IN AN OFFENSIVE CATEGORY?

It was Frank Robinson who best described the time–honored problem of finishing second when he said, "Close doesn't count, except in horseshoes and hand grenades." But it was Mel Ott—he of the hitting style that looked as if he were lifting his right foot from a batter's box paved with glue and employing his bat as if it possessed the blasting power of a grenade—who came the closest to a league championship the most times in one offensive category. Ott, who hit 511 home runs during his playing lifetime—including 323 in one ballpark—won the National League home–run crown three times outright (1936, 1938 and 1942), shared it three years (1932 with Chuck Klein, 1935 with Rip Collins, and 1937 with Joe Medwick), and finished second a record seven times: 1929 and 1931 to Klein, 1935 to Wally Berger, 1939 to Johnny Mize, 1941 to Dolf Camilli, and 1943 and 1944 to Bill "Swish" Nicholson. Those who finished close–but–no–cigar the second most times in an offensive category are Willie Mays and Cap Anson, who both were runners–up four times for the National League batting titles (Mays in 1955, 1957, 1958, and 1960 and Anson in 1880, 1882, 1886, and 1887).

NAME THE ONLY MEMBERS OF THE 3,000–HIT CLUB WITH LIFETIME BATTING AVERAGES BELOW .300.

In some attic somewhere lies the remains of a yellowing newsclip, circa 1897, looking almost as if it were writ in the hieroglyphics of a long–lost society, recounting the feat of a 45–year–old Cap Anson driving a ball out over the infield and becoming the first man in baseball history to attain what had theretofore been thought unattainable, 3,000 hits. Anson, who had achieved his 3,000 hits without a 200–hit season—only one of two members of the 3,000–hit club without benefit of such a season—the other, Carl Yasztremski suddenly became a national figure, one who stood alone atop a hill from which he could look down on the rest of the baseball world, "The Heroic Legend of Baseball." But others had already taken up their bats and would soon be scaling the same heights. The second man to make it was Honus Wagner on June 19, 1914. Then it was Lajoie, then Cobb and the names began coming faster than signs on the San Diego freeway. And by the end of 1985, when Rod Carew finally reached what had almost a hundred years before been thought to have been unreachable, the number of those 3,000 hits stood at 16. But there was no written guarantee with those 3,000 that the player hitting them got an automatic .300 average. Three of those 16 ended their careers somewhat short of what has come to be another so–called "magic" number, the .300 lifetime batting average: Carl Yastrzemski with 3,419 hits and a .285 average, Lou Brock with 3,023 hits and a .293 average, and Al Kaline with 3,007 hits and a .297 average.

THE 3,000 HIT CLUB

PLAYER	# OF HITS	YEAR PASSED 3,000	LIFETIME AVERAGE
Pete Rose	4,204	1978	.304
Ty Cobb	4,191	1921	.367
Hank Aaron	3,771	1970	.305
Stan Musial	3,630	1958	.331
Tris Speaker	3,515	1925	.344
Honus Wagner	3,430	1914	.329
Carl Yastrzemski	3,419	1979	.285
Eddie Collins	3,311	1925	.333
Willie Mays	3,283	1970	.302
Nap Lajoie	3,251	1914	.339
Paul Waner	3,152	1942	.333
Rod Carew	3,053	1985	.328
Cap Anson	3,041	1897	.334
Lou Brock	3,023	1979	.293
Al Kaline	3,007	1974	.297
Roberto Clemente	3,000	1972	.317

WHAT BATTER TOOK THE MOST YEARS TO WIN HIS FIRST BATTING TITLE?

The batting title is one of baseball's biggest pearls. But to most batsmen, it remains an elusive treasure, one they have as much chance of possessing as they would have of opening an oyster with a baseball bat. Some rookies have won it, like the Federal League's Benny Kauff in 1914 and the American League's Tony Oliva half a century later, and even some second–year players like Pete Reiser in 1941 and Al Kaline in 1955. But for most of the other 10,000 players who have come to bat in the major leagues, not only was the batting title beyond their abilities, but their grasp as well—no matter how many years they played. It took Charlie Gehringer no less than 14 years in the big leagues to climb to the top of the batting mountain, winning his first, and only, batting crown in 1937 with a .371 average.

But even the man they called, "The Mechanical Man" has to take a back seat to the man who took the most years to win his first batting title: Al Oliver. Oliver hit .331 in 1982, his first year with the Montreal Expos after spending his previous 14 with the Pirates and the Rangers. Oliver, whose license plate once read, "Al Hits," proved he could. He was an overnight success with Montreal, even if it had taken him 15 years to get there.

Stan Musial won a batting title in his 16th year in the majors and Ted Williams in his 17th, but their batting titles merely filled out their already flowing plates of titles on the half-shell. Musial had a total of seven batting titles and Williams an even half dozen. For Oliver it was his first, the longest it has ever taken any batter to win his first batting title, 15 years.

WHAT PLAYER HAS HIT HOME RUNS IN THE MOST MAJOR LEAGUE PARKS?

The last two decades have seen a building boom, of sorts, in the majors, with franchise-after-franchise replacing their old stadia, viewing them as tired duennas rather than municipal monuments to great memories. In their place have sprung up cookie–cutter molds that go by the name of new ballparks. Added to this proliferation of new stadia, popping up everywhere like spring crocuses, is the flowering of new franchises. It seems that any home run hitter worth his slugging average can almost inaugurate a new park with a home run. However, one man stands alone in the christening of new stadia. Frank Robinson, who has homered in 33 different ones, one more than Hank Aaron, who hit in 32. During his 21-year-career in both leagues, Robinson hit at least one in every park he played in,—even Jersey City's Roosevelt Stadium, where the Brooklyn Dodger's played 15 home games in 1956 and 1957, one against every visiting club each year and two against the Phillies in '56—with the execption of the Asdtrodome,—Seattle Sicks Stadium and Montreal's Jarry Park. The 33rd, and last, stadium Robinson added to the notches on his home run belt was Pittsburgh's Three River Stadium when he frescoed the ball out of the park in the third game of the 1971 World Series.

WHO WON A BATTING TITLE IN THE ONLY YEAR HE EVER HIT OVER .300?

Reflecting on his 1,091 strikeouts, former Detroit Tiger first baseman Norm Cash mused, "Prorated at 500 at–bats–a–year, that means for two years out of the 17 I played, I never even touched the ball." But Cash, who once came to the plate waving a table leg at the offerings of Nolan Ryan, did touch the ball—and often—in 1961, when he led the American League in hits with 193 and in batting with .361. That was to be the only time Cash ever hit over .300, let alone over .286. This onetime batting champion finished with a lifetime .271, the second-lowest lifetime average for any batting champion compared to Snuffy Stirnweiss' .268.

WHO WAS THE ONLY LEFT-HANDED THROWING, RIGHT-HANDED HITTING PLAYER EVER TO WIN A BATTING TITLE?

Baseball has disgraced no man. Unfortunately, a few men have disgraced baseball, none more so than Hal Chase. Chase was a brilliant, left-handed fielding, right-handed hitting first baseman with few peers as a fielder. He was believed by some to have invented the 3–6–3 double play, although a large body of contemporary opinion touts Fred Tenney as the first first baseman to go from first-to-second-to-first for the double play. It was suggested by many that Chase also thought left-handed as well, even if he batted right-handed. His "corkscrew mind," it was hinted, was used to perfect the fine art of throwing baseball games for fun and profit as easily as he threw to second. Chase had started his career as a youth in the outlaw leagues of California and fallen in with gamblers, an association he was to share for the remainder of his career. That career saw him play eight-plus years for the New York Highlanders—even managing them for a little over a year after he had personally engineered shoving George Stallings off the managerial gangplank.

But despite his other shortcomings, Chase gained a fine reputation as the finest-fielding first baseman in the majors while he was with the Highlanders. This reputation made his many errors all the more unexplainable. Chase was hardly a team player, and when the Federal League formed in 1914, he jumped quicker than a claim jumper, seeking to gain his fortune with the new league. He also gained something else, a second reputation for skulduggery. When the Federal League disbanded no American League team would touch him. But Garry Herrmann, president of the Cincinnati Reds and one of the triumvirate that controlled baseball, bought his contract for the 1916 season. And even while manager Christy Mathewson suspected Chase's loyalty, Chase would go on to win the 1916 National League batting title with a .339 average, his highest mark in the majors. Two years and many hearings into his activities later, Chase would go to the New York Giants in 1919, where he would spend his last year in organized ball setting the groundwork for the infamous Black Sox fix in that year's World Series. And when, at the end of the year, he was silently mustered out of baseball for unspecified reasons, Hal Chase took with him all his secrets, his corkscrew mind, and the dubious distinction of having been the only left–handed throwing, right–handed hitting player ever to win a batting title.

Throughout the years the majors have seen a handful of left–handed throwing, right–handed batting players, none of whom were ever to win a batting title. These include Jimmy Ryan, Patsy Donovan, Edward "Pop" Tate, John Cassidy, and Warren Carpenter—all of whom played before the turn of the century—and Rube Bressler, Johnny Cooney, Paul Strand, Carl Warwick, Cleon Jones, and Rickey Henderson in modern times.

WHO IS THE ONLY BATTER TO HIT HOME RUNS OFF BOTH A FATHER AND HIS SON IN THE MAJORS?

Of the 20 father–son pitching combinations in the majors since 1900, only two, the Bagbys and the Colemans, have won 50 games each, with the Colemans working a total of 25 years in the majors between them. But one other father–son pitching tandem tied the Colemans in that number of years of pitching service in the majors. The Lees, Thorton and Don, during that term of service both came up against Ted Williams. Thorton faced Williams in Williams' first year in the majors, 1939, and served up a fast ball to Teddy Ballgame on September 19, 1939, one of his 31 rookie homers. Son Don faced Ted at the tail end of his long career, September 2, 1960, and fed Ted one of the last home runs of his career, one of the 29 he hit in his last year in the majors, a record for last–year players.

WHO WAS THE ONLY NON–PITCHER IN MAJOR LEAGUE HISTORY TO PLAY 10 YEARS AND BE NOT ABLE TO "HIT HIS WEIGHT"?

Remember how it was as a kid when you played baseball on the corner lot with kids named "Fats" and "Stinky" and traded insults that sounded like, "So's your old man!" and, "Your mother wears combat boots!"? And the cruelest cut of all to any kid trying to play was the jibe, "You can't hit your weight!"? Well, there was one man in baseball history who couldn't, hard as that is to imagine for any man who doesn't look like what Jack met at the top of the beanstalk. Nonetheless, for 11 years a catcher named Bill Bergen tried valiantly and just couldn't hit his weight—and his weight was only 184 pounds. Playing, or trying to play, for the Cincinnati Reds and Brooklyn Dodgers between 1901 and 1911, Bergen batted less than his weight in no less than six years (1901, 1902, 1904, 1906, 1908, and 1909) and over his 11–year–career, or what passed for same, he came to bat a total of 3,028 times and managed only 516 hits, a lifetime average of just .170.

Since 1900, others weighed in the batting balance and found wanting, with a minimum of 250 at–bats a season, include: John Bateman, who, in 1967 batted .190 for the Houston Astros, 20 pounds below his weight; Dick Billings of the 1973 Texas Rangers, who weighed 195 and hit only .179; Glenn Borgmann of the 1975 Twins who hit .207, three pounds below his listed weight; and Chris Cannizzaro—called "Canzoneri" by Stengel, maybe because Chris's batting average reminded Casey of the former lightweight—who hit .183 in 1965 while with the Mets, seven pounds below his weight. And then there were the four players with 500 AB's in one season and batting average below 200; Lave Cross (1912), Jim Levey (1933), Frank Crosetti (1937), and Tom Tresh (1962). But none of these batting lightweights comes close, even on a Celsius basis, to matching Bill Bergen who "couldn't hit his weight" for 11 long years.

WHAT TWO PLAYERS HIT HOME RUNS IN THEIR TEENS AND IN THEIR FORTIES?

Back in the 1970s the advertising firm of BBD&O—which Jack Benny always suggested, "sounded like someone falling down the stairs"—was trying mightily to come up with an advertising campaign for one of their clients' products, a bourbon. And, as often occurs in large firms, a meeting was convened to discuss the possibilities. Only in advertising they don't call them meetings, they call them "brain-storming sessions." And so it was that one of the many people hunched around the table, doodling on his pad for inspiration, or anything that worked as an alternative word for "bourbon," suddenly looked up and suggested two names with a ring to them and that rhymed with bourbon: Emil Verban and Deanna Durbin. And that was as far as the idea got. Nobody ran it up the proverbial flagpole and nobody saluted. In short, the idea was less a storm than a drizzle and mercifully blew over.

But the names Verban and Durbin, as dissimilar as they are in everything but their rhyming quality, can undoubtedly be brought back to go with the answer to this question. For the two players to hit home runs in their teens and their forties are Cobb and Staub, providing the second line for their ditty if BBD&O is still interested. Ty Cobb became the first—and, until 1984, the only—player to have home runs in his teens and in his 40s, having hit a total of two over two seasons while still under the age of 20 and another six in the years 1927 and 1928 after he had passed his 40th birthday. Rusty Staub, the party of the second part, hit six home runs in 1963, while still a teenager, and then joined Cobb as the only other man to hit home runs as both a teenager and as an elder statesman when he connected on September 25, 1984. Staub added one more in his last year to bring his figures to six as a teenager and two as a man who finds life begins at 40; Cobb, contrary as he always was, had two as a teenager and six as a 40–year–old. Not quite Verban and Durbin, but it'll scan.

NAME THE ONLY SIX CATCHERS TO HAVE 100 RUNS AND 100 RUNS BATTED IN IN THE SAME SEASON.

Catchers have always been described in catchall phrases, like, "team quarterback," or, "on–the–field manager," or any one of a nest of platitudes that all pay tribute to their abilities behind the plate. But rarely does anyone think to pay tribute to their batting abilities, conveniently overlooking the fact that two of them have won batting titles: Bubbles Hargrave and Ernie Lombardi. In fact, Lombardi has been so overlooked that even the Hall of Fame has overlooked this lifetime .306 player with 17 years service. However, even Lombardi, who could hit the ball into next week even if he had trouble running for the moment, never put together a season in which he scored 100 runs and had 100 Runs Batted In. But six others did: Mickey Cochrane, 1932, 118 runs and 112 RBI's; Yogi Berra, 1950, 116 and 124; Roy Campanella, 1953, 103 and a league–leading 142 RBI's; Johnny Bench, 1974, 108 and a league–leading 129 RBI's; Carlton Fisk, 1977, 106 and 102; and Darrell Porter, 1979, 101 and 112.

WHO HIT BEHIND THE TWO GREATEST HOME-RUN HITTERS OF ALL TIME?

Japan has long been known not only as the Land of the Rising Sun, but of the setting baseball star as well. Starting with the grand tours to Japan of all-star teams back in the 1930s, baseball became our most important export, with names like Babe Ruth and Lefty O'Doul becoming as familiar to Oriental fans as they were to their Occidental counterparts. However, while their legend stayed in Japan, the players didn't. It remained for former Chicago White Sox pitcher Joe Stanka to make both his presence and his future felt in Japan, becoming one of the first to play in the Japanese League in 1959. And once Stanka pulled the cork, the former Major Leaguers began flowing to Japan, Larry Raines, George Altman and Dick Stuart, among others, exporting their talents—with Stuart becoming the first to use his round-trip ticket to return to the Majors after his tour of duty in the Japanese League.

Another of the eight players who used their round-trip ticket to return to play in the Majors after playing in Japan was Davey Johnson. In 1973, as a member of the Atlanta Braves, Johnson had tied Rogers Hornsby's all-time home run record for second baseman with 42—with one more thrown in for good measure as a pinch-hitter. And on the night of April 8, 1974, Johnson was in the sixth position in the batting order when Hank Aaron, hitting fourth, drove one of Al Downing's fastballs into the Braves' bullpen for his 715th home run, establishing himself statistically as the greatest home run hitter in baseball history. The next year saw Johnson playing on the Yomiuri Giants of Tokyo and batting fourth in the line-up directly behind Sadaharu Oh, then on his way to the all-time, all-time record of 868 homers. And when Johnson returned from Japan to close out his career with the Phillies and the Cubs in 1977 and 1978, he would return with the honor of being the only man to hit behind the two greatest home run hitters in baseball history—Hank Aaron and Sadaharu Oh.

WHO IS THE ONLY GRANDFATHER EVER TO HIT A MAJOR LEAGUE HOME RUN?

The normal custom for a spanking new granddad is to hand out cigars. But then again, Stan Musial was anything but normal. Especially as a hitter, where, crouched in a position that looked like a little kid peeking around the corner of a door jamb, he would turn, as slowly as the door itself, and then, setting his sights on the ball, put his bat in action, 475 times during his long 22–year–career in Cardinal red, driving the ball to parts unknown. The next–to–last time he ever did so came on September 10, 1963 in his first appearance at the plate after his daughter–in–law, Mrs. "Dickie" Musial, had delivered a bouncing baby grandson to the new Old Granddad, his son, "Dickie," named after his minor league manager Dickie Kerr, the ex-White Sox pitcher. Batting against Glen Hobbie of the Cubs in the first inning of the night game at Busch Stadium, Musial celebrated his good fortune by driving one of Hobbie's offerings into the right field stands, his 11th homer of the year and 474th of his career—giving Musial not only the honor of being the only grandfather ever to hit a major league home run, but also, with 475 lifetime homers, having the most home runs without ever leading his league in that category.

WHO WAS THE ONLY PLAYER TO HIT EIGHT HOME RUNS IN ONE PROFESSIONAL GAME?

Baseball lore has it that Jim Thorpe, as a minor leaguer, once hit three home runs in one game in three different states—claiming that while a member of a team in Texas he hit one over the right field fence into neighboring Arkansas, one into deep center in Texas, and the other God–Knows–Where. But that story bears the same relationship to truth as those tales concerning Santa Claus and the Easter Bunny.

However, down in the Texas League, where legends are as big as all outdoors—and where Gene Rye of the Waco team in the Texas League once hit three home runs in one inning, August 6, 1930—one player once hit eight home runs in one game. And that tale is the truth, and, as such, bears retelling.

On June 15, 1902, Corsicana hosted Texarkana in a Texas League game. And, on that day, a young 19-year-old catcher named Jay "Nig" Clarke went to bat eight times, and eight times, devouring the ball just as easily as an overstuffed banquet guest would devour a plate of roast beef—and just as quickly—he wrote his name into the record books and his legend in gravenstone by hitting eight balls out of the park. In the process he drove in 16 runs and hit for a total of 32 total bases, all professional records. And Corsiciana, then in the midst of a 27-game winning streak, a professional record which still stands for all of baseball, went on to win a "squeaker," 51-3—a score so unbelievable that Western Union operators, unable to believe their eyes and ears, transmitted it as "5-3." Texarkana was so driven by the loss, that by midseason they had dropped out of the Texas League, never to return.

As for Clarke, he would make it to the majors three years later and spend a total of nine years and 506 games behind the plate for no less than five teams. However, sad to relate, in his 1536 major league at-bats, he would amass the meagre total of six home runs—or two less than he did in one afternoon when he became the only player to hit eight home runs in one professional baseball game.

WHEN DID TED WILLIAMS HIT HIS ONLY INSIDE-THE-PARK HOME RUN?

Gil McDougald, Yankee infielder, once explained the Williams Shift to a reporter whose pencil was poised, thusly: "If it works, it's a great play. If it doesn't, it's a horseshit play." And the Williams shift was sometimes both. A defensive ploy which moved all the infielders around to the right side of the infield, leaving third unprotected, with the outfielders adjusted accordingly, the Williams Shift was first used by Cleveland Indians' manager Lou Boudreau in 1946. The shift came into being after a particularly frustrating game on July 14 that saw Boudreau set the all–time record with five extra base hits in one game only to have his team lose 11–10 on Williams' three home runs. "I was so damned mad at seeing my hits wasted that I came up with that cockeyed Williams Shift on the spur of the moment," Boudreau was to explain later, still hurting from the thought. "I knew he could pop short flies to left for doubles all day long, but I was willing to take that chance as long as somebody else had to drive him in," Boudreau rationalized.

And it was against the Williams Shift that "The Thumper" hit his only inside–the–park home run. On September 13, 1946, two months after the Shift had first been employed against him, Williams came to bat with the entire Indian defense amassed over toward the right side, almost as if they were huddling together for protection against the upcoming rain storm. With left fielder Pat Seerey moved far over to center in spacious Municipal Stadium, the supposed dead pull hitter caught an outside pitch from pitcher Red Embree in the first inning and stroked it over the outstretched glove of Seerey, a short squat figure of a man who most resembled a fire plug. As Seerey huffed and puffed after the ball, Williams did the same around the bases, finally collapsing on home just ahead of Seerey's tardy throw, the only time he ever hit an inside–the–park home run in his career. It was also the 38th and last for Williams that year. And, most importantly, it won the game 1–0—one of five times Williams would provide the game–winning home run in a 1–0 game, a major league record that would later be tied by Bobby Bonds—and clinched the pennant for the Red Sox, their first pennant since 1918.

The Williams Shift was soon adopted by the rest of the league and was still in vogue a year later, when, during a game in Fenway Park, a dwarf wandered down from the stands to cover third base. "Hell, nobody else was," he was to say later as he was being removed.

WHO WERE THE LAST SET OF BROTHERS TO BOTH HIT HOME RUNS IN THE SAME GAME?

Lightning rarely strikes twice in the same place. Or so it has been rumored. But you couldn't prove it by baseball where more than a few times brothers have caught proverbial lightning in the same bottle, two of them hitting home runs in the same game. The first time brothers made hitting home runs a family act came on September 4, 1927 when both Lloyd and Paul Waner hit home runs off Cincinnati pitcher Dolf Luque in the fifth inning. The Waners were to repeat their unique act twice more, the last time coming on September 15, 1938 when both tagged New York Giant pitcher Cliff Melton for homers in the fifth inning—the last time Lloyd ever hit a home run. Other home–run–hitting brothers joined in the act, with the Ferrell brothers (Wes and Rick) hitting them against each other on July 19, 1933, Tony and Al Cuccinnello hitting them against each other on July 5, 1935, and Joe DiMaggio and his little brother Dom hitting home runs against one another on June 30, 1950. Then, proving that brothers who play together stay together, at least so far as hitting home runs is concerned, the Aarons (Hank and Tommie) accomplished the feat three times, the Congiliaro brothers (Tony and Billy) twice, and the Alous (Matty and Felipe) the first time, then to make sure it was a real family affair, Jesus and Matty the second. The last set of brothers to both use their bats as lightning conductors in the same game were the Nettles, Graig and Jim. On September 14, 1974, Graig got to Mickey Lolich of the Tigers in the first inning and brother Jim reciprocated with a home run off Yankee pitcher Pat Dobson the next inning, the 14th and last time brothers ever hit homers in the same game.

ALPHABETICALLY, STARTING WITH AARON FOR "A" AND BANKS FOR "B," WHO WAS THE LAST OF THE ALL–TIME HOME RUN LEADERS?

Just as the old question of the 1930s, "Alphabetically, who was the last of the Seven Dwarfs?" seeks the last in a list, (in this case Sneezy) so too does the question, "Alphabetically, starting with Aaron for "A" and Banks for "B," who was the last of the all–time home–run leaders?" seek the last in a list—this time the list of all–time home–run leaders by letters of the alphabet. The answer, alphabetically speaking, is Gus Zernial, the man known as "Ozark Ike," who hit 237 roundtrippers in his 11 years in the majors, more than any other player whose name begins with the letter "Z." And ends the list that started with Aaron as the "A" and Banks as the "B" who hit more all–time home runs than any other player whose name begins with either "A" or "B."

The 25–man list, going from "A" to "Z"—with no one ever having played major league ball whose name marks the roster with an "X"—leaves out many of those on the all–time home–run list who do not also lead their letter of the alphabet in homers. These include Frank Robinson (fourth with 586) behind the "R" leader Babe Ruth; Mickey Mantle (sixth with 535), Willie McCovey (tied for eighth with 521), Eddie Mathews (tied for 11th with 512), and Stan Musial (15th with 475). They all rate behind the leader of the "M" squad, Willie Mays. Mike Schmidt (18th with 458) and Duke Snider (tied for 20th with 458) are behind the all–time "S," Willie Stargell. And Billy Williams (19th with 426) comes behind Ted. Only one of those on the alphabetical all–time list is a nineteenth–century player. He is Joe Quinn, who, with 30 homers, is the all–time leader for "Q," beating out second–place Jamie Quirk, who had but 15.

ALPHABETICAL LIST OF ALL-TIME HOME-RUN HITTERS

A–Hank Aaron	755	N–Graig Nettles	368
B–Ernie Banks	512	O–Mel Ott	512
C–Orlando Cepeda	379	P–Tony Perez	377

D–Joe DiMaggio	361	Q–Joe Quinn	30
E–Darrell Evans	318	R–Babe Ruth	714
F–Jimmie Foxx	534	S–Willie Stargell	475
G–Lou Gehrig	493	T–Frank Thomas	286
H–Frank Howard	382	U–Willie Upshaw	88
I–Monte Irvin	99	V–Mickey Vernon	172
J–Reggie Jackson	530	W–Ted Williams	521
K–Harmon Killebrew	573	Y–Carl Yastrzemski	452
L–Greg Luzinski	307	Z–Gus Zernial	237
M–Willie Mays	660		

WHO WAS THE LAST MAJOR LEAGUE BATTING CHAMPION TO BAT OVER .400?

Perhaps the greatest achievement in all of baseball is that of batting .400, an accomplishment that cements its performer's greatness and establishes a depth of affection and hold on fans that not only outlasts the player's career, but oftimes his life as well. Over the years only 18 men have ever transcended that magical barrier, and only eight of those in modern times: Ty Cobb (three times), Rogers Hornsby and George Sisler (twice), Nap Lajoie, Joe Jackson, Harry Heilman, Bill Terry, and, of course, the last to hit .400 in the majors, Ted Williams, who, in 1941, hit .406 without benefit of the sacrifice fly rule.

But the last Major league batting champion to bat over .400—albeit not in the majors—was Tony Oliva, who, in his first year in professional ball, 1961, hit .410 for Wytheville, Va. in the Appalachian League. Three years later, in 1964, Oliva followed that feat by winning the first of his three American League batting championships and, in the process, set a major league record for most total bases by a rookie with 374 total bases.

WHAT FATHER–SON DUO HAS THE MOST COMBINED HOME RUNS?

After agreeing to appear on a radio talk show with sportscaster Jack Buck, Yogi Berra was handed a check for twenty–five dollars made out to "Bearer." Berra studied the check for a second and then said to Buck, "Jack, how long have you known me? How the hell could you spell my name like that?" But Berra was the "bearer" of something more than that twenty-five dollar check. He was also the bearer of a son named Dale, and between them, the Berras smote more home runs than any other father–son tandem in history, a total of 405, with Berra *père* hitting 358 and Berra *fils* adding 47. But what the Berras are not an answer to is the trivia question that circulated around New York watering holes after son Dale was acquired from the Pittsburgh Pirates in December of 1984. The question in question posed the stickler, "Which is the first father–son duo to be on the same team as manager and son?" The answer presupposed the Berras. Sorry, wrong bearers. The answer is the Macks, Connie and his son, Earle, who played all of five games over three years while his father managed the Philadelphia A's.

The most home runs for a grandfather–grandson combination are the 24 hit by Shano Collins, who played for the Chicago and Boston Sox from 1910 through 1925 and his grandson, Bob Gallagher, who put in four seasons in the early 1970s: 22 for the old granddad and only two for his grandson.

3rd Inning
The Pitchers

WHAT PITCHER PITCHED THE LONGEST IN THE MAJORS BEFORE HIS FIRST 20–GAME SEASON?

Unlike Wes Ferrell, who burst upon the major league scene with four straight 20–game seasons in his first four full years, the only pitcher ever to do so, many pitchers have had to bide their time, waiting for that 20–game season to come. If it ever did. One of those who waited . . . and waited . . . and waited . . . was Tommy John. John broke in with the Cleveland Indians in 1963, his first two years in the majors less worthy of an analysis than an autopsy; his combined record was 2–11. After two years with the Tribe, John was traded to the Chicago White Sox in a three–team trade where he diligently plied his own trade for the next seven years, averaging 11+ wins a year. But still nary a 20–game season in the carload. After the 1971 season, John was sent packing to the Los Angeles Dodgers in exchange for Richie

("Don't call me 'Dick'") Allen, and, by his third season in Dodger Baby Blue, he was well on his way to a 20–game season when he ruptured a ligament in his throwing arm during a game on July 1, 1974, an injury that necessitated a postseason operation. Out the entire 1975 season, John continued to pitch batting practice. But some sensed that his arm was up for retirement long before John had thought about it for himself. John even saw the bittersweet humor in the situation, commenting, "When they operated on my arm, I asked them to put in a Koufax fastball. They did . . . Mrs. Koufax's." The determined leftie kept everlastingly at it and finally rejoined the Dodgers in time for the 1976 campaign, a campaign that saw him go 10 and 10. And then, in 1977, Tommy John posted a 20–7, 14 years after he had first come onto the major league scene and the longest any pitcher has ever had to wait for his first 20–game season.

NAME THE PITCHER OFF WHOM PETE ROSE HIT HIS ONLY CAREER GRAND SLAM HOME RUN.

Pete Rose, according to writer Larry Merchant, "Got his base hits in the present and thought in the past." But one time this man, who became the most prolific base hitter of all with his 4,192nd base hit September 11, 1985 off San Diego's Eric Show, hit in the future as well. Few remember his home run with the bases filled on July 18, 1964, his only career grand slam. What was notable about it was not just that it was his only career grand slam, but who Rose picked to hit it off: Philadelphia Phillies pitcher Dallas Green, his future manager. But then again, managers have not been treated all that well by their future charges.

Back in 1914 a young pitcher for the Baltimore Orioles, Babe Ruth, made his professional debut on April 22nd against Buffalo's Eastern League entry. One of those who roamed where the Buffalos played was their second baseman, Joe McCarthy, Ruth's future manager. Ruth hardly treated McCarthy with the deference supposedly commanded by a future manager. He held McCarthy hitless.

Perhaps the greatest dual act of disrespect to a manager took place during the 1946 season when Pee Wee Reese of the Dodgers and Eddie Waitkus of the Cubs both established club fielding marks, breaking those held by their managers at the time, Leo Durocher and Charlie Grimm.

WHO WAS THE ONLY PITCHER TO THROW A NO-HITTER AGAINST THE HOUSTON COLT .45s?

For the first three years of their expansion life, 1962, 1963 and 1964 the Houston club in the National League called itself the Colt .45s, in honor of the gun that won the West. But when the Colt company demanded something that sounded like an honorarium for the use of its name, the Houston team and its parsimonious owner, Judge Roy Hofheinz, demurred. Instead, they opted to find a new nickname for their team, coming up with the Astros. But during the short existence of the Houston Colt .45s, they were the victims of one no-hitter which was thrown by San Francisco Giant pitcher Juan Marichal on the afternoon of June 15, 1963. Not incidentally, it was also the first no-hitter ever thrown by a Hispanic pitcher, providing Marichal with his own special niche in the Baseball Trivia Hall of Fame, where he joined Dolph Luque, who was the first Hispanic pitcher to win 20 games in a season (1923) and the first to win a World Series game (1933).

WHAT TWO LEFT–HANDERS HAD THE MOST WINS FOR ONE CLUB IN ONE SEASON?

It seems that throughout the course of history left–handers have always gotten the fuzzy end of the lollipop. How else can you explain the fact that the minority in any legislative assembly always sits on the left side of the aisle? Or that the French word for "left" is *gauche* which has come to mean "bent out of shape" or "awkward of style"? Baseball was no different in its formative years, treating left–handers as if they were recent releases from leper colonies. In fact, during the evolutionary period of organized baseball, left–handers were noted for their complete absence. Then, in 1870, two left–handers—Edward Pinkham of the Eckfords of Brooklyn and Charley Pabor of the Unions of Morrisiana—became part of the baseball landscape. But it remained for Cincinnati Red Stocking Robert Mitchell to become organized baseball's first left–handed pitcher in 1877: the first stone to hit the water, breaking in never–ending circles. By 1900 left–handers had won a begrudging degree of acceptance. Still, they *were* different, and to label them as different from "normal players" the right–handed world coined the term "southpaws," a term originating with the fact that almost all ball parks were built with home plate in the West so that the left–hander's throwing arm was facing South.

In 1901 Connie Mack, manager of the newly formed Philadelphia team in the American League, called up two pitchers—both, not incidentally, southpaws—to serve as trace horses for his so–called "White Elephants," Rube Waddell and Eddie Plank. Together Waddell and Plank formed a disparate pair and pairing. Waddell, was a man–child who alternately roamed the diamond and the saloon with equal ease and gave southpaws a reputation for zaniness that would remain theirs throughout the ages. This reputation caused fellow southpaw and zany Bill Lee years later to lament, "What do you expect from a northpaw world?" On the mound Waddell was fast, both in his delivery and in what he delivered, challenging batters with his fastball and managers with his eccentricities—even going so far as to call in his outfielders with the bases loaded and no outs and to strike out the side on nine pitches. Plank was drab in comparison, a comparison that would dim his greatness and submerge his name. A Gettysburg College graduate, Plank was contemplative and disciplined, pitching with control of both himself and his opponent. Plank could open up a batter like a flowering rose for his off–speed pitches. Together, this oil–and–water duo dominated the American League for four years, winning a total of 190 games between them from 1902 through 1905. And in 1904 the pair won 51 games between them, a feat they repeated, like the watering of last year's crop, in 1905 to set the record for the most wins by any two left–handers on the same club in one season. Ironically, Connie Mack would find yet another pair of left–handers in the 1920s and in 1931 the two, Lefty Grove and Rube Walberg, rewarded him with another 51–game season for two lefties, tying the record.

NAME THE TWO PITCHERS WHO GAVE UP HOME RUNS TO BABE RUTH IN HIS 60–HOME–RUN SEASON AND HITS TO JOE DIMAGGIO IN HIS 56-GAME STREAK.

Thirty–four pitchers gave up home runs to Babe Ruth to account for his record–setting 60 homers back in 1927. Fourteen years later, forty–three different pitchers gave up hits to Joe DiMaggio during his record–setting 56–game hit streak. Two of the pitchers can be found on both lists of donors, Ted Lyons and Lefty Grove, both members of the Baseball Hall of Fame. Lyons, who came up to the White Sox directly from Baylor University in 1923, threw home run number 54 to Ruth at Yankee Stadium on September 18, 1927 and gave up two singles to DiMaggio on July 13, 1941 to keep his streak alive at 52 games. Grove, who came up to the Philadelphia A's in 1925, gave up home run number 57 to Ruth at Yankee Stadium on September 27 and, in his last year in baseball, gave up a single to DiMaggio on May 25, 1941, the 11th game in DiMaggio's streak.

WHAT PITCHER WON 19 GAMES MORE TIMES THAN ANY OTHER PITCHER?

Although the magic number of wins for a pitcher is 20—many pitchers getting there and no further, such as Paul "Daffy" Dean who won 19 his first two years in the majors and never approached the total again—one man, Jim Bunning, came close to the magic circle no less than four times. One of those four seasons was 1964 when his 20th win—or that by his alternating starter Chris Short—would have meant the difference between a pennant and baseball's greatest stretch collapse, one that saw the Phillies take on the look of an immense sail going limp in a change of wind losing 10 of their last 11 games. And the pennant.

WHO WAS THE FIRST MODERN PITCHER TO RELIEVE HIMSELF ON THE MOUND?

This question can be misinterpreted in much the same way that an old historical marker which proclaims proudly, "Lee's Last Movement" on the road between Washington, D.C. and Richmond, Va., can be misread by charter members of the Flat

Earth Society. But in an age where variations on the theme of relief pitching are almost endless, a pitcher may not only come to the aid of another pitcher, but even come to his own relief—or more indelicately, can relieve himself on the mound.

To see just how a pitcher could relieve himself on the mound, consider the following scenario: in a game between the Chicago White Sox and the Boston Red Sox at Fenway Park on May 15, 1951, manager Paul Richards of the White Sox stage–managed a change of positions called a "Rare Hill Maneuver" by *The Sporting News*. Going into the bottom of the ninth and leading 7–6, the first batter, right–handed relief pitcher Harry Dorish was scheduled to face left–handed hitter Ted Williams. Despite the fact that Dorish had pitched a scoreless eighth, Richards called "time" and waved in his ace lefty, Billy Pierce, moving Dorish over to third and taking his third baseman, Hank Majeski, out of the lineup. Richards' strategy worked—at least momentarily—as Pierce retired Williams on a pop–up. Richards then removed Pierce, brought Dorish back in to face the right–handed hitting cleanup batter and put Floyd Baker in at third. However, a walk and a pair of singles enabled Boston to tie the game in the bottom half of the ninth, and Dorish had to hold on, struggling to a 9–7 win in 11 innings. He was the first pitcher in modern history to relieve himself on the mound.

Emboldened by his success—a success that saw the so–called "Go-Go" Sox win 20 of 25 games in May of 1951 and attain the lofty position of first place—Richards went on to pull the same ploy three more times! Once in 1953, bringing in a new pitcher and moving Pierce over to first, then bringing him back after one batter; and two more times in 1954, when he moved right–hander Sandy Consuegra to third for one batter and another time when he moved left–hander Jack Harshman over to first for one batter. However, his greatest discovery that day in May, 1951 might have been that, as good players go, his third baseman Hank Majeski would have to go. The very next day, May 16, 1951, Richards bought Bob Dillinger from the Pittsburgh Pirates, a move that made his third baseman less expendable and made his having his relief pitcher relieve himself on the mound a less frequent occurrence.

There was one other time when a pitcher relieved himself on the mound that bears inclusion, it being a part of baseball history. On August 31, 1968, Steve Blass started the game for the Pittsburgh Pirates against the Atlanta Braves, got the leadoff batter out, and then was moved to left field as Elroy Face took the mound for the last time in a Pirate uniform. Face, already sold to the Detroit Tigers, was making his 802nd lifetime appearance in one uniform, tying the all–time record held by Walter Johnson. Face retired the only batter he faced, Felix Millan, then left the game and Blass resumed his pitching chores as the Pirates went on to win, 8–0. Later, during the same game, it was announced officially that Face had been sold to the Tigers.

WHO WAS THE FIRST—AND LAST—PITCHER TO FACE PETE GRAY IN THE MAJORS?

The year was 1945 and the winds of World War II were still gusting over the country. Everyone, athletes included, was caught up in the draft. With a manpower vacuum facing them, the major leagues had taken on the look of a Turkish bazaar, stocking itself with men to fill out their rosters who would have done Emma Lazarus proud. They were the lame, the halt, and the nearly blind: in short, the 4Fers. In fact, everybody but the Singer Midgets had been conscripted for what had been the National Pastime before World War II supplanted it, and there were rumors that four or five teams were attempting to sign even *them* to contracts.

To fill its depleted ranks, the 1944 American League pennant winners, the St. Louis Browns ferchrisake, had bought a one–armed outfielder named Pete Gray from the Memphis Chicks. Gray, in 1943, had hit .333 and stolen a record–tying 68 bases on his way to becoming the Southern Association's Most Valuable Player. Some claimed he was added insurance for the

Brownies in their efforts to repeat as champions. Other more cynical critics, noting that despite leading their league in wins the Browns had been dead–last in attendance, claimed Gray was there as a mere promotion, an attention and attendance builder. But whatever the motives in signing him, because he had but one arm and popular prejudice runs in favor of two, Gray was destined to become more a curio than a contributor.

His debut came on the afternoon of April 18, 1945 against the Detroit Tigers and their fireballing left–hander Hal Newhouser, who was coming off an incredible 29–9 year. Newhouser faced Gray three times and retired him three times, getting him on an infield grounder to shortstop Jimmy Webb, on a called third strike (one of only 11 times that year that Gray would strike out, the second lowest total in the majors), and on a sinking line drive that was caught by centerfielder Roger "Doc" Cramer with a tumbling, shoestring catch. Newhouser was replaced in the seventh by Les Mueller, who gave up Gray's first major league hit, an infield single. But Gray's presence in the lineup underwhelmed St. Louis fans, only 4,167 showing up to cheer on the American League champions and oftimes sounding like one hand clapping. Some five months and 150 games later, the Tigers and the Browns were once again locked in combat, this time with the American League pennant at stake. It was the last game of the year, the one won by Hank Greenberg's grand slam home run in the top of the ninth to give the Tigers the pennant. And the winning pitcher this time around was the same Hal Newhouser who had lost the season opener. Facing Gray in the eighth inning, Newhouser forced Gray to hit into a fielder's choice as he advanced Lou Finney into scoring position in his last major league game at bat. This time the Browns and Gray were watched by 5,582 of the faithful.

Hal Newhouser should be remembered for more—much more—than merely as the man who was the first and last pitcher to face Pete Gray in the majors. For during a five–year span, from 1944 through 1948, the man known as "Prince Hal" won more games over five years than any pitcher since 1930 and is the only eligible back–to–back winner of the Most Valuable Player Award (besides Roger Maris) not to be enshrined in the Hall of Fame.

WHO WAS THE FIRST BLACK PITCHER IN THE MAJOR LEAGUES TO THROW A NO–HITTER?

Just as Lindbergh was the 19th man, not the first, to cross the Atlantic—albeit the first to fly solo—so too did Sam Jones gain instant immortality by becoming the first black pitcher in major league history to pitch a no–hitter, even if he was the 121st pitcher and the second named Sam Jones to do so. Pitching for the Chicago Cubs against the Pittsburgh Pirates on the afternoon of May 12, 1955, the man called "Toothpick Sam," because he had a toothpick surgically implanted in his cheek, walked the first three men to face him in the top of the ninth and then struck out Dick Groat, Roberto Clemente, and Frank Thomas on a total of 12 pitches to become the first pitcher to hurl a no–hitter in Wrigley Field since the double no–hit game between Fred Toney and Jim Vaughn some 38 years previous. Jones was to repeat history, of a sort, by becoming the second black pitcher to throw a no–hitter as well, throwing a rain–shortened seven–inning no–hitter against the St. Louis Cardinals on September 26, 1959. He was on his way that year toward becoming the first black pitcher to lead his league in Earned Run Average. Jones was also the first black pitcher to be on the opposite end of a no–hitter, Warren Spahn's second no–hitter on April 28, 1961.

WHO WAS THE ONLY PLAYER TO PITCH AMBIDEXTROUSLY IN A PROFESSIONAL GAME IN THIS CENTURY?

Those few remaining graybeards who have not yet been run over by trolley cars may well remember Tony Mullane, the nineteenth-century pitcher who pitched both left and right–handed during his 13–game career to save wear and tear on his arm. He pitched so well, in fact, that he won 285 games, the most ever by a pitcher eligible to be in the Hall of Fame who is not so enshrined. Other nineteenth-century switch–pitchers included Larry Corcoran, John Roach, and Icebox Chamberlain. But modern fans have not had the rare treat of witnessing a pitcher during this century throwing from both sides of the mound in a game. There have been ambidextrous players such as Paul Richards, Edd Rousch, Jorge Rubio, and, of more recent vintage, Lee Mazzilli, who was described by Met General Manager Joe McDonald as "unable to throw either way." There has been even an ambidextrous U.S. president, Harry Truman, who would open every season with two ceremonial first pitches—both right– and left–handed. Some pitchers have thrown batting practice both left– and right–handed, pitchers like Dave "Boo" Ferriss, Cal McLeish, and Early Wynn. Wynn admitted that he would occasionally lose his subjects during batting practice, laughing as he said, "They quit because I didn't have control," a remark made all the more laughable when one considers that its source was the man who stands second in all–time walks with his natural hand.

The closest modern fans have come to witnessing a pitcher in action from both sides of the mound in a major league game came in 1973 when Tug McGraw toyed with the idea. He even went so far as to search out umpire Tom Gorman before the game and ask, "If a man's on second and I drop my glove, can I pick him off right–handed?" Gorman, according to writer Red Foley, who was within earshot, replied, "Better not try it. I don't think the League would allow that, it's a false move." And so McGraw never did.

However, someone did try it. Bert Campaneris, in his first year of professional ball playing for the Florida State League's Daytona Beach entry, took the mound as a relief pitcher on August 13, 1962 and pitched right–handed to the right–handed batters and left–handed to the left–handed batters for an inning plus, the only man to switch–pitch in this century.

WHO WAS THE LAST PITCHER TO STEAL HOME?

Bob Gibson stole 13 bases in his 17–year career, one more than Truett "Rip" Sewell, for the all-time base stealing record for pitchers. And yet neither of these two ever stole home, something accomplished by no less than 28 pitchers—an even more astonishing fact when one considers that public energy number one, Lou brock, who holds the all-time record, never stole home. The last time this implausible act occured was September 1, 1963, when St. Louis Cardinal pitcher Curt Simmons victimized his old team, the Philadelphia Phillies. Racing home from third on a squeeze play that went awry, Simmons beat Chris Short's wide throw and Bob Oldis' tardy tag for one of the two stolen bases in his 20–year career—still 11 behind Gibson's record.

STEALS OF HOME BY PITCHERS:

NATIONAL LEAGUE

July 15, 1902	John Menafee, Chicago	5th Inning vs. Brooklyn
August 8, 1903	Joe McGinnity, New York	3rd Inning vs. Brooklyn
April 29, 1904	Joe McGinnity, New York	7th Inning vs. Boston
September 12, 1911	Christy Mathewson, New York	3rd Inning vs. Boston
May 22, 1912	Leon Ames, New York	5th Inning vs. Brooklyn
June 28, 1912	Christy Mathewson, New York	4th Inning vs. Boston
July 22, 1913	Slim Sallee, New York	3rd Inning vs. St. Louis
April 16, 1916	Sherry Smith, Brooklyn	3rd Inning vs. New York
June 23, 1916	Tom Seaton, Chicago	5th Inning vs. Cincinnati
July 26, 1918	Bob Steele, New York	7th Inning vs. St. Louis
August 9, 1919	Jim Vaughn, Chicago	8th Inning vs. New York
September 3, 1919	Dutch Reuther, Cincinnati	4th Inning vs. Chicago
July 27, 1920	Jesse Barnes, New York	6th Inning vs. St. Louis
May 4, 1921	Dutch Reuther, Brooklyn	5th Inning vs. New York
September 23, 1943	Johnny Vander Meer, Cincinnati	5th Inning vs. New York
April 20, 1946	Bucky Walters, Cincinnati	6th Inning vs. Pittsburgh
May 26, 1955	Don Newcombe, Brooklyn	9th Inning vs. Pittsburgh
September 1, 1963	Curt Simmons, St. Louis	2nd Inning vs. Philadelphia

AMERICAN LEAGUE

August 2, 1904	Frank Owen, Chicago	3rd Inning vs. Washington
May 7, 1906	Bill Donovan, Detroit	5th Inning vs. Cleveland
April 27, 1908	Frank Owen, Chicago	9th Inning vs. St. Louis
June 13, 1908	Ed Walsh, Chicago	7th Inning vs. New York
June 2, 1909	Ed Walsh, Chicago	6th Inning vs. St. Louis
August 30, 1909	Eddie Plank, Philadelphia	2nd Inning vs. Chicago
August 27, 1910	Jack Warhop, New York	6th Inning vs. Chicago
July 12, 1912	Jack Warhop, New York	3rd Inning vs. St. Louis
July 14, 1915	Urban Faber, Chicago	4th Inning vs. Philadelphia
August 7, 1916	Reb Russell, Chicago	3rd Inning vs. Boston
August 24, 1918	Babe Ruth, Boston	2nd Inning vs. St. Louis
July 8, 1921	Dickie Kerr, Chicago	7th Inning vs. New York
April 23, 1923	Urban Faber, Chicago	4th Inning vs. St. Louis
August 15, 1923	George Mogridge, Washington	12th Inning vs. Chicago
September 17, 1944	Joe Haynes, Chicago	8th Inning vs. St. Louis
August 29, 1947	Fred Hutchinson, Detroit	3rd Inning vs. St. Louis
June 2, 1950	Harry Dorish, St. Louis	5th Inning vs. Washington

WHO WAS THE ONLY MAN TO SERVE UP A HOME-RUN BALL TO TOMMIE AARON BUT NOT TO HANK?

One of baseball's stock trivia questions over the last decade has been: "What brothers hold the combined record for most home runs?" The answer, "The Aaron brothers with 768," leaves purists, as well as those with little sense of humor for trivia, garnished with a curve and livid. Their residual sense of memory is offended and they look for all the world as if the questioner had just pointed out a severe case of hoof–and–mouth disease in their personal favorite of the herd. They would have the answer be the DiMaggios whose total of 573—the same number of homers smote by Harmon Killebrew—gives them second place and a close–but–no–cigar mention.

Hank, who was to hit a record 755 homers, personally decimated National League pitching for 21 years, owning certain pitchers—such as Don Drysdale whom he touched for 17 round–trippers—as if they were his own personal property. His domination was so complete that one opposing pitcher was even moved to lament, "Trying to sneak a ball past Hank Aaron is like trying to sneak a sunrise past a rooster." Even the Dodgers' Rex Hudson, who snuck into his only major league game on July 27, 1974, was touched for home run number 726 by Aaron the merciless.

But one pitcher, Jack Hamilton of the Philadelphia Phillies and New York Mets, was able to escape Hank's scorched–earth devastation. Unfortunately, Hamilton could not escape brother Tommie, who hit the first of his 13 major league home runs off Hamilton on April 26, 1962. Hamilton would also add another footnote to baseball when, on August 18, 1967, as a member of the California Angels, he beaned Tony Conigliaro, bringing Tony's career to an early end.

WHAT PITCHERS HAVE BEATEN EVERY ONE OF THE EXISTING 26 TEAMS IN THE MAJORS?

Not unlike the man who had to loosen his belt continuously to ingest more and more food, baseball has taken to expanding its own horizons by seating more and more cities at its own exclusive dinner table. And, in a manner similar to the French who perpetuate the quaint custom of hiring a "13th man" to flesh out their dinner parties so as not to have the same number of participants as sat at the Last Supper, baseball since 1977 has gone to extremes to accommodate a number other than 13 at its own table: 14 in the American League and 12 in the National. Therefore, it should come as no surprise that the expansion to 26 teams should beget a trivia question all its own, namely those pitchers who have beaten each and every one of those 26 teams.

Beating each and every one of the 26 teams in the majors presupposes both that a pitcher pitched for at least two clubs in each league and has been active since 1977, two facts that hold true for five of the six pitchers on the list—Doyle Alexander, Gaylord Perry, Mike Torrez, Rick Wise, and the last to do so, Don Sutton, who beat Milwaukee in 1985 to complete his personal sweep. However, the exception to the rule is Tommy John, who only pitched for the Los Angeles Dodgers in the National League. But, by beating the Dodgers in the second game of the 1981 World Series, John joins the select group—with an asterisk.

WHAT BOSTON RED SOX PITCHER WAS ON THE TEAM'S ROSTER THE LONGEST?

When one considers all the great pitchers the Boston Red Sox has had on its rosters down through the years—pitchers like Lefty Grove, Smoky Joe Wood, Mel Parnell, Ellis Kinder, Herb Pennock, Ernie Shore, and Dutch Leonard amongst others—it is mind–boggling to note that Ike Delock, with 11 years, is the pitcher with the greatest number of years' service as a Red Sox pitcher. But, as Jimmy Durante once said, "Them's the conditions that prevail." Delock pitched for the Red Sox from 1952 through 1963 and won 83 games for the BoSox against 72 losses.

WHO IS THE ONLY PITCHER TO HAVE OVER 3,000 STRIKEOUTS AND UNDER 1,000 WALKS?

There are only nine pitchers who have accomplished the Herculean feat of striking out 3,000 men during their major league careers—Nolan Ryan, Steve Carlton, Gaylord Perry, Walter Johnson, Tom Seaver, Don Sutton, Ferguson Jenkins, Bob Gibson, and Phil Niekro—and only one whose control has been so pinpoint perfect that he walked fewer than 1,000 men: Ferguson Jenkins. In his 19–year career, Jenkins struck out 3,192 men and walked just 997. The only under–over pitching act which can even compare with Jenkins' strikeout–walk record is that of "Parisian" Bob Caruthers, the only man to win over 200 games and lose under 100, his 218–97 won–lost record begetting him the highest won–lost percentage in baseball history, .692.

WHO WAS THE ONLY PITCHER WITH 20 WINS TO WIN THE ROOKIE OF THE YEAR AWARD?

Since the Baseball Writers Association of America introduced the Rookie of the Year Award in 1947—originally an across–the–board award for both leagues given to Jackie Robinson in 1947 and Alvin Dark in 1948, then split apart in 1949 and awarded to Don Newcombe of Brooklyn in the National League and Roy Sievers of St. Louis in the American—no less than 21 pitchers have won.

However, only one, Bob Grim of the New York Yankees in 1954, was a 20–game winner. The others ranged from a high of 19 for Jack Sanford, Gary Peters, and Mark Fidrych to a low of seven for Steve Howe. On the other side of the mound, four rookie pitchers with 20 did not win the Rookie of the Year

Award: Gene Bearden of the 1948 Cleveland Indians, who lost to Dark; Alex Kellner of the 1949 Philadelphia A's, who lost to Sievers; Harvey Haddix of the 1953 Cardinals, who lost to Junior Gilliam; and Tom Browning of the 1985 Cincinnati Reds, who lost to Vince Coleman of the St. Louis Cardinals.

WHAT 20-GAME WINNER WON THE FEWEST GAMES THE REST OF HIS CAREER?

For most pitchers, the winning of 20 games is a harbinger of great things to come. However, for a small number, it was less a harbinger than the end of the line, their 20–game season serving as their valedictory to baseball. Back in the 19th century, no less than 10 pitchers never won another game after their 20–game seasons. The reasons were almost as varied as the pitchers themselves: Illness (Charlie Ferguson); the demise of the league (Hank O'Day, Players' and Bill Sweeney, Union Association); or simply because their skills had suddenly deserted them (Terry Larkin). However, it is not the 19th century pitchers who can be counted on to give us the answer to this question, but their 20th century counterparts, five of whom were to win 20 games, and then, like the Raven in Poe's *magnum opus,* "Nevermore" win another game the rest of their careers. And the reasons for the sudden extinction of their once-brilliant flame were almost as varied. For Amos Rusie, a fireballing righthander who had won 20 or more games eight consecutive seasons,it was a holdout which kept him out of the game for two years. Returning briefly in 1901 after being traded for a young pitcher named Christy Mathewson, Rusie found his fire was gone. And soon so was he, ending his days as an attendant at his beloved Polo Grounds. For Claude "Lefty" Williams and Eddie Cicotte, it was the ignominy of the 1919 "Black Sox" scandal—or as Cicotte was to say, "I have played a crooked game and I have lost"—and being banished from baseball after the 1920 season, a season that saw both win 20 games. For Sandy Koufax, it was the constant pain from his arthritic left elbow which caused him to quit in 1966 at the top of his game. And for the fifth, a 20–year–old pitcher named Henry Schmidt, it was homesickness. Schmidt, who hailed from Brownsville, Tex.,won 21 games for the 1903 Brooklyn Dodgers and then never pitched another game in the Majors, claiming that he would rather stay home and not travel than go through another Major League season—thus leaving Schmidt with a lifetime Major League record of 21-13, all of which came in his rookie, and only, year in the Majors.

WHO ARE THE ONLY THREE BATTERS TO HIT EXTRA–BASE HITS OFF THE "EEPHUS PITCH?"

Some pitchers are identified by their pitches almost as readily as a band is identified by its musical signature. Mention the Hesitation Pitch and one thinks of Satchel Paige; the Folly Floater and it's Steve Hamilton; the Fadeaway and it's Christy Mathewson; the Screwball and it's Carl Hubbell; the . . . Oh, you get the idea. But perhaps the most famous pitch of all was the Eephus Pitch, a frustrating pitch that was thrown off the toes and released from back of the head and which held its line of flight to the plate owing to the terrific backspin it had. And the possessor, really the patenter of that famous pitch was Truett "Rip" Sewell, who threw it, and threw it often, for the Pittsburgh Pirates during most of the 1940s.

The Eephus Pitch got its name in an exhibition game back in 1943 between Sewell's Pirates and the Detroit Tigers in Munsey, Ind. Sewell had come in to pitch the last three innings and with two out in the last inning, rookie phenomenon Dick Wakefield came to the plate. Sewell got two quick strikes on Wakefield and then looked in for the sign from Al Lopez. Lopez called for Sewell to throw his change of pace. Instead, he threw a change of space. Wakefield stared at it, started to swing and stopped. Then he started to swing again, finally going through with it, swung, missed and fell down. While his teammates, "laughed like anything," Sewell was accosted by newsmen who wanted to know what he called whatever it was. And while Sewell was thinking up a fanciful name, the mere label Blooper hardly doing it justice, reserve outfielder and full-time kibitzer Maurice Van Robays said it was, "an eephus ball." When pressed as to exactly what in the hell, "an eephus ball was," Van Robays just shrugged and said, "Eephus ain't nothing . . . and that's what it was, nothing." And from that day on, the Eephus Pitch lived.

The Eephus Pitch was a larger–than–life blooper that almost made batters want to throw away their bats, clench their fists, and punch it over the fence with their bare hands. Still, it presented an inviting target. One day in 1943 a young rookie named Lonnie Goldstein sat on the Cincinnati bench watching Sewell retire Red after Red with his Eephus Pitch. Through clenched teeth Goldstein said to nobody in particular, "I'll knock that ball down his throat . . . ." Manager Bill McKechnie overheard his raw young rookie's boast and sent him up to pinch hit, all the while the dignified McKechnie was laughing out loud. With the count at 2–2, Lopez again gave sign to Sewell to let go with the Eephus Pitch and Sewell complied, throwing his famous 15–foot blooper. Goldstein, "swung from Port Arthur," according to Sewell, "went into the clubhouse, and hasn't been seen since."

Some disdained swinging at the ball at all. Whitey Kurowski merely spat tobacco juice at it as it came down from on high and crossed the plate. But a few, a rare few, had some success. Ron Northey, the Phillies' outfielder, caught one of "Rip's" bloopers and ripped a triple to right center field one afternoon in Philadelphia. And Stan Musial smote one into the screen in Sportsman's Park for a double on another. But most couldn't hit it. "Only one in 15," said Sewell, with a wicked chuckle in his voice.

However, one batter did hit it, and hit it very well, the only time an Eephus Pitch was ever hit out of the ball park. That moment came during the 1946 All–Star Game in Boston. Sewell had come in to pitch for the National League, which was then in the process of being beaten up pretty badly by the American League, the score standing at 8–0. Sewell was greeted by singles off the bats of Snuffy Stirnweiss and pitcher Jack Kramer, and, after a sacrifice fly by Sam Chapman had brought the ninth run home, decided, "enough was enough," and determined to, "have fun," regaling his opponents, and the fans, with his Eephus Pitch. But Vern Stephens met it for a single. And now, with Boston slugger Ted Williams at bat, Sewell decided to match strength with strength. Williams followed the first one for a strike. Now Williams, giggling, asked Sewell to throw yet another. Sewell, mixing a little deviltry with a little so's–your–old–man mentality, threw his famed pitch and Williams, timing not only his swing but also moving up a stutter–step in the batter's box, thumped it. The ball hasn't stopped yet, thus enabling Williams to join Northey and Musial as one of the only three batters ever to get an extra base hit off "Rip" Sewell's famous Eephus Pitch.

WHO ARE THE ONLY TWO BOSTON RED SOX LEFT–HANDERS EVER TO PITCH A NO–HITTER IN FENWAY PARK?

Before he was scheduled to pitch at Fenway, Yankee pitcher Lefty Gomez would sit outside the stadium in a phone booth, all the better, he insisted, to acclimate himself to Fenway's unfriendly confines for left–handed pitchers. And ever since Fenway Park opened on May 12, 1912, that friendly left–field wall, known to one and all as "The Green Monster," has posed a threat to any left–hander who dares take the mound. As an afterthought, Boston management raised a screen above the Monster in 1936 to save balls—and save Huddleston's windows as well. But by then it had become an inviting target for any and all right–handed batters, some of whom, like Keltner, Clift, Hayes, Gordon, and Laabs, had taken direct aim at it. Right–handed pitchers had little or no difficulty taming the wall. Walter Johnson pitched his only no–hitter in its shadow. But lefties throughout the years have fared less well. Even poorly. And even though great left–handers have taken their turn in "The Fens," only three have come away with no–hitters, two of them Red Sox: Dutch Leonard on August 30, 1916 against the St. Louis Browns, Yankee George Mogridge against the Sox on April 24, 1917, and most recently, Melvin Lloyd Parnell—better known as just plain ol' Mel—against the Chicago White Sox on July 14, 1956; all three of whom brought the green monster to its knees.

WHO IS THE ONLY PITCHER TO HURL NO–HITTERS AT BOTH THE 50–FOOT DISTANCE AND FROM THE 60–FOOT, 6–INCH DISTANCE?

From a pitching standpoint, the line of demarcation came in the early 1890s when the distance from the pitcher's mound to home plate was changed from 50 feet to the current 60 feet, 6 inches—a change, some of baseball's romantics hold, that came when a groundskeeper misunderstood the instructions to move the pitcher's rubber to something that sounded like "sixty–six" and plunked the pitching rubber down at its present distance. And only one pitcher straddled both distances—and eras—with no–hitters: Ted Breitenstein, who threw one at the old distance in 1891 and one at the current distance in 1898.

Ironically, the 50 foot no-hitter came in Breitenstein's first major league start. This made the man they called, "The Young Amateur" one of four men to pitch no–hitters in their first major league starts. The others were: Bumpus Jones (1892), Red Ames (a five–inning no–hitter in his debut in 1903), and Bobo Holloman (1953).

Breitenstein also holds another distinction, thereby earning three places in the Trivia Hall of Fame. Along with Bill Monbouquette, Breitenstein has the longest last name—12 letters—of any pitcher ever to throw a no–hitter.

WHAT PITCHERS WITH AT LEAST 20 DECISIONS HAD THE BEST WON–LOST RECORD AGAINST THE NEW YORK YANKEES?

Throughout most of the last seven decades, Yankee bats have been to pitchers what Kryptonite was to Superman and the True Cross was to Dracula, alien objects which rendered them powerless. But two pitchers, both of whom toiled against the Yankees back in the pre Murderer's Row days, were effective. Very effective. Those two pitchers, both left–handers, were Dickie Kerr, who pitched for the White Sox for four years and had a 14–4 record against the Yankees for a won–lost percentage of .778, and George Herman "Babe" Ruth, who pitched for the Red Sox for four full seasons and part of two others and won 17 while losing only five against New York for a won–lost percentage of .773, the pitcher with at least 20 decisions to have the best W-L record against the Yankees.

The right–hander with the best won–lost record against the Yankees was of more recent vintage. He was Frank Lary, "The Yankee Killer," who had a 28–13 mark against the Yankees for a .684 percentage.

WHAT MAJOR LEAGUE PITCHER PICKED OFF THE FIRST TWO BATTERS TO REACH BASE AGAINST HIM?

Tommy Harper, a two–time base–stealing champion who knew whereof he spoke, once opined, "The best pitchers have the worst moves to first. Probably because they let so few runners get there." But others, rather than merely sending out a telegram to their managers reading, "Have runners on base. Please advise," have had to employ a pick–off move as part of their pitching arsenal, a strategy designed both to compensate for their lack of other skills and as a retaliatory tactic against those who have had the audacity to actually stake claim to a base against them. When Nick Altrock was with an outlaw team in Los Angeles back in 1901, he deliberately walked the first seven batters to face him in one game and then promptly picked each one of them off at first, offering as his only excuse, "It was the only way I could get those S.O.B.'s out." On August 29, 1883, Guy Hecker of Louisville gave up four hits to John Stricker of the Athletics, but retaliated by picking Stricker off base three times. And Hall of Famer Pud Galvin, then pitching for the Pittsburgh American Association Club, walked the first three Brooklyn batters to face him on the afternoon of September 23, 1886, and then, almost as easily as picking his teeth, picked the three base runners off base.

However, it remained for a modern–day pitcher, Art Mahaffey, to become the first and only Major League pitcher to pick off the first two men reaching base against him. Just called up from the Phillies' Buffalo farm team, Mahaffey made what many considered an idle boast when he predicted that he would pick off the first player to reach base against him in the Major Leagues. Coming in for his first Major League appearance in relief in the seventh inning of a July 30th, 1960, game against the Cardinals, Mahaffey gave up a base hit to Card first baseman Bill White. If those who had heard Mahaffey's braggadocio were laboring under a delusion, they didn't labor long, and in less time than it takes to read this sentence he had fulfilled his prophecy by picking White off first. But Mahaffey wasn't through. The next batter, Curt Flood, got a single. And, almost as if he were echoing an old Al Jolson. "You ain't seen nothin' yet . . ." line, Mahaffey repeated his legerdemain, picking Flood off first as well. It was a one–of–a–kind nonpitching performance.

WHO IS THE ONLY PITCHER TO WIN 20 GAMES IN A YEAR WITH FEWER THAN 30 MOUND APPEARANCES?

When baseball starts handing out its own awards, the award for developing the pitch known as the fork–fingered fastball will undoubtedly be awarded to Ernie "Tiny" Bonham, in much the same manner as the credit for the curveball has been given to Candy Cummings. And yet, Bonham also holds another distinction. He is the only pitcher to win 20 games in a year with fewer than 30 games pitched in. Pitching in 1942, for the New York Yankees, he went to the mound just 28 times, starting 27 games and completing 22 of those for an incredible record of 21–5. The "mostest with the leastest" club also includes another Yankee pitcher, Bob Grim, who, in his rookie year of 1954, became the only pitcher ever to win 20 games with fewer than 200 innings pitched, working but 199 innings in a total of 37 games.

WHAT PITCHER LOST A GAME TWO MONTHS AFTER HE HAD RETIRED?

The story told about Rick Cerrone, the man who mans the information central desk in the Baseball Commissioner's Office, is that one day, a year or so ago, he got a telephone call late in the afternoon. "Hello," said the slightly slurred voice on the other end of the line, sounding as though its owner had already tippled more than one cup of kindness for auld lang syne, "Is thish the Baseball Commishioner's Office . . .?" Rick, so the story goes, held his ground and admitted that it was. Now sure of his quarry, the owner of the voice went on, "Is it possible for a pitcher to both win and lose a suspended game," stopping to punctuate his question with an audible gasp for breath, "if he was traded in the meantime . . ." and then trailed off into something that sounded like a pub song. Rick, dutifully, and let it be known, correctly, answered, "No," all the while thinking only of hanging up and getting back to the business at hand. With hardly a word of thanks, the disembodied voice on the other end, in the guise of a black telephone, said, "Here . . . tell my friend." Now a new voice came over the wire. "Hello . . . we're calling from Philadelphia," it said, as if that made any difference. "What whazzz the answer," it demanded, "Yes or no." It was at this point that the storyteller said that Cerrone, normally a mild–manner man who would rival Clark Kent at his best, snapped "Yes," and hung up, contemplating the amusing scene now taking place some 100–and–a–half miles south between two barroom trivia buffs who were carrying on their minor disagreement about both the answer to the question and what the Baseball Commissioner's Office had told them.

The story, one hurries to inform readers, is not one based in truth. But Cerrone handles hundreds of calls a day. And, in his defense let it be known that he has never been rude to any caller no matter how crude his question. This in stark contrast to Don Larsen, who, when asked about his Perfect Game in the 1956 World Series by someone passing for a sportswriter: "Was that the greatest game you've ever pitched?" merely scowled at the writer for his innocence and ignorance. Anyway, Cerrone admits that he has been asked the question in a more sobering form and assures us that the answer is an unqualified, "No."

But while this improbable set of circumstances can never come to pass, a similar situation can—a pitcher *can* win or lose a game after he has retired. Not a mere reconciliation of a bookkeeping error, such as the addition of one more win to Christy Mathewson's lifetime total some 40 years after he retired, but in an actual game that was suspended. And one did: Jim Hearn in 1959. Hearn, who pitched in the Majors from 1947 through 1959 for the St. Louis Cardinals, the New York Giants and the Philadelphia Phillies, won 109 games and lost 88 during his career. However, it was the game he lost a full two months after he had retired, his 89th, that moves Hearn into the Baseball Hall of Trivia, front and center. 1959 found Hearn toiling for the last–place Phillies in his 13th and final year in the Majors. Where once he had run on a high octane content, his personal gastank was now all but dry. Relegated to the bullpen, Hearn pitched in a total of just six games that year, all in relief. His only two decisions, both losses, came in the games of May 10th and May 11th. In that game of May 10th, Hearn pitched one–and–a–third innings against the Pirates in Pittsburgh, allowing two hits and two runs, both earned, and was on the hook and the book as the losing pitcher when the game was suspended with the Pirates leading 6–4 after 8⅔ innings because of the Pennsylvania Sunday "Curfew Law." The game was scheduled to be resumed for July 21st, the next time the two clubs were to meet. But a funny thing happened to Hearn on his way to that resumption: he was released on May 22nd. And so, by the time the game was completed on July 21st, Hearn was no longer on the roster, instead having returned to Atlanta to sell underwear for the Van Husen Company. And while most baseball records become a tour map to the player's achievements, Hearn's became more, much more, a tour map all the way to Atlanta where he picked up an "L" two full months after he had retired from baseball.

WHAT PITCHER WON THE MOST GAMES IN A YEAR WITHOUT PITCHING A SHUTOUT?

Normally, the story is number nine, standard size. It goes something like this: the pitcher who wins 20 or more games invariably has several shutouts pointing his way like breadcrumbs toward that magic figure of 20. Grover Cleveland Alexander scattered a one–season record 16 along the way toward his 33 wins back in 1916, and Walter Johnson spun a record 110 shutouts along the route toward his lifetime total of 416 wins, more than one for every four victories. However, other pitchers have treated shutouts with all the deference one typically saves for lepers. One, Dave Koslo of the New York Giants, led the National League in Earned Run Average in 1949 without pitching a shutout, the only pitcher ever to lead in ERA without doing so. And pitcher Ron Bryant won 24 games for the San Francisco version of the same with nary a shutout. But the all–time record for wins without a shutout belongs to Bullet Joe Bush, who, pitching for the New York Yankees back in 1922, won 26 games without a shutout to his credit. On the other side of the mound, Virgil Trucks once won five games for the Tigers with three shutouts to his credit—two of them no–hitters—and Karl Spooner won two games for the 1954 Dodgers, both of them shutouts in his first two major league starts.

WHAT PITCHER, IN HIS ONLY MOUND APPEARANCE IN THE MAJORS, WAS THE VICTIM OF A NO–HITTER?

According to one probability study, a no–hitter occurs about once in every 16,000 games. However, one pitcher who suffered from a sharp lack of arithmetic was George Frederick "Peaches" Graham, who, in the only game he ever pitched in the Majors, ran up against one. Graham had appeared for a quick look–see with the Cleveland Indians in 1902, playing in one game at second base and pinch hitting in the other, and had two hits in six at–bats while he was looking. The next time he looked, he was on the mound for the Chicago Cubs on September 18, 1903, facing the Philadelphia Phillies' star pitcher, Chick Fraser. Fraser, showing a profound contempt for his opponent's skills, beat "Peaches" and creamed the Cubs, blanking them without a hit. That was to be Graham's first—and last—appearance as a pitcher in the Majors, as he made some strategic changes in his career strategy and next emerged as a catcher with the 1908 Boston Braves, remaining in the Majors for another five years.

One other pitcher, George Estock, gets an honorable mention in this category. Estock, toiling for the Boston Braves as a relief pitcher in 1951, saw service in 37 games, only one as a starter. The day of his big league debut as a starter, May 6, 1951, was against Pittsburgh's Cliff Chambers, who not only beat Estock and the Braves, but no–hit them in Estock's only Major League start.

WHICH OF PITCHING'S TRIPLE CROWN WINNERS ALLOWED THE LEAST HITS IN THE YEAR IN WHICH HE LED THE LEAGUE IN WINS, EARNED RUN AVERAGE, AND STRIKEOUTS?

Pitching's version of the Triple Crown has been defined as leading the league in victories, Earned Run Average, and strikeouts all in one year. This coupling of pitching's leading categories rivals those three represented by batting's Triple Crown—batting average, home runs, and Runs Batted In. Since the Earned Run Averages were first officially calculated in 1913 in the American League and 1912 in the National, 11 pitchers have won pitching's Triple Crown 20 times, dating from the first modern winner, Walter Johnson in 1913, down through the most recent winner, Dwight Gooden in 1985. And these two Triple

Crown champions, who bookend the list of those who have accomplished the feat since 1913, also lead in two other categories: Johnson, the first winner, leads in allowing the least hits per game, only 6.0 per nine innings; Gooden allowed the least number of hits in the year in which he won the Triple Crown—a total of just 198.

PITCHING'S TRIPLE CROWN WINNERS

NAME	CLUB	YEAR	WINS	ERA	K'S	HITS/ NINE INNINGS	HITS TOTAL
Tommy Bond	Boston, NL	1877	40	2.11*	170	9.0	530
Hoss Radbourn	Providence, NL	1884	60	1.38*	441	7.0	528
Guy Hecker	Louisville, AA	1884	52	1.80*	385	7.0	526
Tim Keefe	New York, NL	1888	35	1.74*	333	6.5	316
John Clarkson	Boston, NL	1889	49	2.73*	203	8.8	589
Amos Rusie	New York, NL	1894	36	2.78*	200	8.7	426
Cy Young	Boston, AL	1901	33	1.62*	158	7.8	324
Christy Mathewson	New York, NL	1905	31	1.27*	206	6.7	252
Rube Waddell	Philadelphia, AL	1905	26	1.48*	287	6.3	231
Christy Mathewson	New York, NL	1908	37	1.43*	259	9.0	285
Walter Johnson	Washington, AL	1913	36	1.09	243	6.0	230
Grover Alexander	Philadelphia, NL	1915	31	1.22	241	6.1	253
Grover Alexander	Philadelphia, NL	1916	33	1.55	167	7.5	323
Grover Alexander	Philadelphia, NL	1917	30	1.86	201	7.8	336
Hippo Vaughn	Chicago, NL	1918	22	1.74	148	6.7	216
Walter Johnson	Washington, AL	1918	23	1.27	162	6.7	241
Grover Alexander	Chicago, NL	1920	27	1.91	173	8.3	335
Dazzy Vance	Brooklyn, NL	1924	28	2.16	262	6.9	238
Walter Johnson	Washington, AL	1924	23	2.72	158	7.6	233
Lefty Grove	Philadelphia, AL	1930	28	2.54	209	8.5	273
Lefty Grove	Philadelphia, AL	1931	31	2.06	175	7.8	249
Lefty Gomez	New York, AL	1934	26	2.33	158	7.1	223
Lefty Gomez	New York, AL	1937	21	2.33	194	7.5	233
Bucky Walters	Cincinnati, NL	1939	27	2.29	137	7.0	250
Hal Newhouser	Detroit, AL	1945	25	1.81	212	6.9	239
Sandy Koufax	Los Angeles, NL	1963	25	1.88	306	6.2	214
Sandy Koufax	Los Angeles, NL	1965	26	2.04	382	8.7	216
Sandy Koufax	Los Angeles, NL	1966	27	1.73	317	6.5	241
Steve Carlton	Philadelphia, NL	1972	27	1.97	310	6.7	257
Dwight Gooden	New York, NL	1985	24	1.53	268	6.4	198

*ERA recalculated by *MacMillan Baseball Encyclopedia*, not official at the time

WHAT 200–GAME WINNER HAS THE HIGHEST LIFETIME EARNED RUN AVERAGE?

Some pitchers approach their chosen profession like condemned men, standing on the pitching rubber with the proverbial cigarette dangling from their lips, eschewing the blindfold before they go into their windup. One of those who pitched that way for 17 years was Earl Whitehill, who, over the course of his career, pitched in 3,565 innings and won 218 Major League games. And yet, while he was toiling for four Major League clubs accumulating his win totals, Whitehill was also amassing a hefty Earned Run Average as well, 4.36—more than two–and–a–half times greater than the pitcher with the best lifetime ERA. That was Ed Walsh, who could manage only 195 wins in 15 years, 23 less than Whitehill despite his obvious greater efficiency. The second highest ERA for a 200–game winner, 3.98 belongs to Louis Norman "Bobo" Newsom, who impressed no one but himself with an ERA almost as commodious as his waistline. Newsom also holds the record for most earned runs given up in a season, 186 in 1938. On the other side of the pitching rubber, Joe Harris, who pitched for the Boston Pilgrims from 1905 through 1907, compiled a record of three wins and 30 losses, but had an ERA of 3.35, according to the *MacMillan Baseball Encyclopedia's* ERA figures—a full run–per–game less than Whitehill.

WHO IS THE ONLY PITCHER TO LEAD HIS LEAGUE IN WINS AND LOSSES THE SAME YEAR?

Twenty–game losers are almost a genetic link with the past when it seemed that almost every year some pitcher or other would lose the magic number—even while winning it. Take the case of George Mullin, for instance. Mullin, pitching for the pennant–winning Detroit Tigers of 1907, just managed to lose 20 at the same time he was winning 20, making him the only 20–game loser to pitch in a World Series. But even then he failed to lead his league in either wins or losses. Mullin's feat was matched by Joe McGinnity in 1901 and, Bill Dineen in 1902. And although neither led the league in victories, Dineen did manage to lead the league in losses with 21, the same number he won. However, there was one pitcher who managed to *both* win and lose more games than anybody else in the league, and it happened within recent memory—1979, in fact. That was the year that knuckleballer Phil Niekro somehow, someway managed to win 21 games and lose 20 for the Atlanta Braves, both league–leading figures, and become the only man to lead his league in both.

NAME THE FOUR PITCHERS TO WIN 20 GAMES IN ONE SEASON SPLIT BETWEEN THE TWO LEAGUES.

Four times in the history of baseball a team has benefited by having a new pitcher join them in *season interruptus* and go on to win a combined total of 20 games. It was almost like getting money from home without writing. The first time it happened was in 1902 when Iron Man Joe McGinnity jumped ship along with his skipper, John McGraw, leaving Baltimore of the American League in the lurch and joining the New York Giants. McGinnity, who already had a 13–10 record with the then seventh–place Orioles, would add eight more of both garden varieties, wins and losses, and wind up with a 21–18 record for the last–place Giants. The next time someone leapfrogged leagues came two years later when Patsy Flaherty was sent apacking by the Chicago White Sox and told to take his 1–2 record with him. Flaherty joined the Pittsburgh Pirates where he added 19 more wins to go with his nine losses, giving him a total of 20–11. The third time a pitcher won 20 spreadeagled across two leagues came in 1945, when the Chicago Cubs, casting around for another pitcher to help them in their pennant drive, latched onto Hank Borowy of the New York Yankees, who was inexplicably waived by the league. Borowy, who had been 10–5 with the Yankees up to July 27, picked up right where he left off with the Cubs, adding another 11 wins and just two defeats to end up with 21–7 and as the starting pitcher in that year's World Series. And the last time a pitcher won 20 games split between two leagues came back in 1984 when the Cleveland Indians sent Rick Sutcliffe to the Chicago Cubs for Mel Hall, Joe Carter, and a minor league pitcher on June 13, 1984. At the time of the interleague trade, Sutcliffe was pitching at a rather uninspired rate, his record just 4–5. But catching fire after the trade, Sutcliffe went 16–1 for a total 20–6, leading the Cubbies to the National League East championship and winning the National League's Cy Young Award, or 16⁄20ths of it at least.

WHO ARE THE ONLY THREE PITCHERS IN BASEBALL HISTORY TO WIN MORE 1–0 GAMES THAN BERT BLYLEVEN?

Colonel Jacob Ruppert, owner of the New York Yankees during their heyday back in the 1920s, used to accost his star right–hander, Waite Hoyt, and, jumping up and down like Rumplestiltskin, demand to know, "What's the matter with you? Other pitchers win their games 9–3, 10–2. You win yours 1–0. Why don't you win your games like the others?" But even though Waite Hoyt would win his share of 1–0, and even a few 2–1 games, games that Ruppert admitted, "Make me nervous," he was far off the pace of the all–time leader, Walter Johnson, who won 38 games by a 1–0 score—and, not incidentally, also lost 27 by a 1–0 score, the anemic Senators unable to score for him, or anyone for that matter. Second behind Johnson's all–time record is Grover Cleveland Alexander, who turned in 17 1–0 victories during his career. And third, Eddie Plank with 15, Federal League included. And behind those three is Bert Blyleven, who has pitched no less than 14 1–0 games over his 16–year career.

WHAT PITCHER HAS LOST THE MOST PLAY–OFF GAMES IN BASEBALL HISTORY?

The first play–off game of any sort was the replay of the famous 1908 Merkle Boner game in which Fred Merkle, upon seeing the winning run cross the plate in the person of fellow Giant Moose McCormick, on Al Bridwell's hit turned tail and ran for the clubhouse instead of touching second. Chicago Cub second baseman Johnny Evers, who, only two weeks before appealed a similar play to umpire Hank O'Day when Pittsburgh

Pirate base runner Warren Gill failed to touch second on the game–winning hit, this time invoked the help of umpire O'Day again. And this time he got it, along with the ball, which had been passed back and forth in the outfield like a parcel nobody wanted to pay the postage on. In the re–play–hyphen–play–off, the Cubs beat the Giants and won the pennant, with Christy Mathewson losing to Three Finger Brown.

During the next 76 years there have been no less than 16 other play–off games, with six of those coming as a grouping in 1981 when baseball tried to extricate itself from the mess made of its schedule by the strike. The other play–offs in baseball history have come in 1946 (the St. Louis Cardinals over the Brooklyn Dodgers in two games), 1948 (the Cleveland Indians over the Boston Red Sox in one game), 1951 (the New York Giants over the Brooklyn Dodgers in three games), 1959 (the Los Angeles Dodgers over the Milwaukee Braves in two games), 1978 (the New York Yankees over the Boston Red Sox in one game) and 1980, (the Houston Astros over the Los Angeles Dodgers in one game.) And three times the same pitcher has lost play–off games. The man who was three times unlucky was number 13, Ralph Branca, who lost the first game of the 1946 play–offs to the Cardinals and the first and third games of the 1951 Giants, the last coming on Bobby Thomson's famous Shot Heard 'Round the World.

WHAT PITCHER ALLOWED THE MOST RUNS IN ONE INNING?

Technology usually doesn't reverse itself. But in the case of one man, Francis Joseph "Lefty" O'Doul, it did. Originally signed by his hometown San Francisco Seals in 1917 as a pitcher, O'Doul first saw his major league light of day in 1919 with the Yankees. But over the next three years he was thought to have little diamond presence and less of a future as manager Miller Huggins used him but five times in two seasons. And then all in relief for a team that had no need for relief of any kind, its pitching staff being among the greatest in history. Optioned to San Francisco in 1921, O'Doul put together a 25–6 year and came back up to the Yankees for one last look–see. But he was barely seen before being sent apacking to the pitiful and pitiable Boston Red Sox in a trade which would fetch the Yankees Joe Dugan. It was while he was with the Red Sox on July 7, 1923 that O'Doul had a day that was well worth the forgetting. Taking the mound in the sixth inning to face the Cleveland Indians, an inning that was to go down in history as The Indian Massacre, O'Doul faced 16 Cleveland batters and gave up 13 runs in Boston's 27–3 loss, a negative Major League record that still stands. It was all too clear that O'Doul was now a finished pitcher, in the truest meaning of the phrase.

Visions of what might have been and what was, merged. The next year, O'Doul announced to his manager at Salt Lake City that he was no longer a pitcher—a moot point—and was now an outfielder. He made his point, hitting .392 in 140 games and started a second career as an outfielder, one good enough to bring him back up to the Majors again. This time around all O'Doul did was lead the league in batting twice, with .398 for the 1929 Phillies and .368 for the 1932 Dodgers, and wind up with a lifetime .349 batting average for his 11 years in the majors—the second highest for any man not in the Hall of Fame behind Joe Jackson. O'Doul's turnaround was similar to that of Tris Speaker, who started his career as a pitcher for Cleburne of the North Texas League, lost six straight, his last a 22–4 defeat, and became an outfielder too.

In later years, O'Doul would become known as the Man in the Green Suit, a color that suited him as well as he suited baseball when he became the self–appointed Baseball Ambassador to Japan and managed the San Francisco Seals to three Pacific Coast League championships. But one of Lefty O'Doul's contributions that is most frequently overlooked is his role of batting instructor for *Pride of the Yankees,* taking Gary Cooper under his wing during the shooting of the film and teaching that gangling and uncoordinated movie star how to hit left–handed, something Lefty did very well himself, but, ironically, never for the Yankees.

WHO IS THE ONLY PITCHER EVER TO OFFICIALLY LEAD HIS LEAGUE IN BATTING?

Most modern pitchers would prefer to walk through a mine field than come to bat. But it wasn't always thus. Several of the old–time pitchers would rather talk about their batting than their pitching. And for good reason. Babe Ruth aside, some pitcher-pitchers have established more–than–respectable batting averages, with George Uhle, who pitched 17 years with Detroit and Cleveland, hitting at a .288 average over his career, the highest lifetime batting average of any pitcher–as–batter. Others who could win a game with their bat as well as with their arm included Red Lucas who hit .281; Wes Ferrell, who had a .280 average and a record 38 homers for a pitcher; Don Newcombe, who compiled a .271 batting average and in 1955 outhit his teammates, the World's Champions, with a .359 average in 117 at bats; Red Ruffing, who not only had a lifetime .269 average over 22 years, but is one of the only three Hall of Famers in the list of most pinch–hits in a career; and Walter Johnson, who had the best single–season average for a pitcher with .433 in 1925 when, at the age of 37, The Big Train had 42 hits in 97 times at bat. But one pitcher who could beat a team in more ways than one was Guy Hecker, who in 1886, not only won 27 games for the Louisville club in the American Association, but also led the league in batting with a .342 average, getting 118 hits in 345 at–bats, the only pitcher in history ever to do so.

WHAT PITCHER GAVE UP THE MOST HITS IN ONE GAME?

Sometimes victors are by victory undone. Take Eddie Rommel, one of baseball's best pitchers in that very short period of time between the leave–taking of Walter Johnson and the entry of Lefty Grove. Generally credited with bringing the knuckleball to baseball, Rommel toiled diligently and hard for an aggregation that could only aspire to the term "team," the Philadelphia A's of the early 1920s. They were so decimated that all that was missing from them was a note from their mothers attempting to explain their emotional absence, the direct result of Connie Mack having broken up his great team in 1914 after losing the Series to the Braves, financially unable to do battle with the new Federal League in the bidding wars for his stars. The A's had what amounted to permanent possession of last place when a strapping right–hander with a knuckle ball in the person of Eddie Rommel joined them in 1920 and won seven and lost seven for a team that won just 48 games all season.

In 1921 Rommel raised his number of wins to 16 out of a total of 53 for the entire team, but lost a league–leading 23 as the A's floundered and finished in eighth place for the seventh straight year. In 1923 both Rommel and the A's improved. Rommel won a league–leading 27 games—only one of two times that a pitcher has led the league in losses one year and come back to lead in wins the next with both totaling over 20—and the A's finally relinquished their hold on last place. Suddenly Rommel's was a stock that had trebled in value as over the following three years he averaged 19 wins a year, all the while Connie Mack was putting together the nucleus for his future great teams. But finally Rommel's arm began to give way under the strain, and, finding himself surrounded by the likes of Lefty Grove, Rube Walberg, and "Moose" Earnshaw, he became, at best, a spot pitcher, used mainly in relief. And it was in relief that Rommel made his niche in the Trivia Hall of Fame. The date was July 10, 1932, and Philadelphia, with no Sunday baseball in Pennsylvania because of the existing Blue Laws, had a scheduled Sunday game in Cleveland, a one–game series. Mack, once again in a financial pinch despite having just won three straight pennants, took a skeleton crew to Cleveland for the one game. It was worse than a blunder; it was a crime—especially for the dozen or so Athletes who had to endure one of the longest games in the history of baseball. And one of the strangest. With but two pitchers to call on, Rommel drew the short straw as Mack decided to use the younger one, Lew Krausse, holding Rommel in reserve. Reserve came quicker than anticipated as the Indians greeted Krausse with three runs in the first inning. Rommel took over in the second and pitched the next 17 innings as each team kept everlastingly at it. When the smoke had cleared and the damage was assessed, the total was 18 runs and 25 hits for the A's to 17 runs and 33 hits for the Indians. And of those 17 runs and 33 hits, Rommel had given up "just" 29 hits in his 17 innings—including a record for one game of nine by Indian shortstop Johnny Burnett—and would have allowed more had it not been for three great catches by center fielder Mule Haas, the most hits ever given up in one game. It was to be Rommel's last major league win and last major league appearance, a helluva price to pay for making history of any kind, even of the negative variety.

NAME THE ONLY FIVE PITCHERS WHO HAVE HAD PERFECT GAMES THROUGH 26 BATTERS.

If it wasn't Willie Shakespeare who said, "Merely this and nothing more," it well could have been. Or any one of the five pitchers in Major League history who retired the first 26 batters to face them, only to lose their Perfect Games—and instant immortality—to the 27th and final batter. The first time a pitcher lost his Perfect Game to the 27th man came on July 4, 1908, when George "Hooks" Wiltse of the New York Giants set down the first 26 men he faced in order, only to lose his bid for eternal fame when, with the count 1–2, opposing pitcher George McQuillan of the Phillies swung at an apparent third strike only to have plate umpire Cy Rigler call it a ball. Unnerved, Wiltse hit McQuillan on the arm with his very next pitch. Wiltse would go on to win 1–0 in 10 innings on an extra inning no–hitter with McQuillan having been the only man to reach base. The second time came on August 5, 1932, when Detroit Tiger ace Tommy Bridges set down 26 in a row, only to come up against Washington Senator pinch hitter Dave Harris, who wasted no time in wasting Bridges' Perfect Game, hitting the first ball thrown for a single. The third near–Perfect Game came on June 28, 1958, when Chicago White Sox left-hander Billy Pierce retired the first 26 men and then came afoul of Washington Senator pinch hitter Ed FitzGerald who spoiled his chance for greatness by doubling down the right field foul line. The next–to–last time someone flirted with immortality came on September 2, 1972, when Cincinnati Red pitcher Milt Pappas, with 26 straight men under his belt, walked the 27th, pinch hitter Larry Stahl of the Padres, on a 3–2 pitch, before retiring the next man for his no–hitter. After the game, commenting on the controversial call by plate umpire Bruce Froemming, all Pappas could do was angonize: "He had a chance to become famous as the umpire in the 12th perfect game in baseball history, and he blew it." The final almost–was was on April 15, 1983, when Detroit's Milt Wilcox held the Chicago White Sox to no hits, no runs, no men–on–base for 26 batters, only to have the 27th, Jerry Hairston, break it up in the ninth with two out—the fifth and final time a pitcher lost his Perfect Game to the 27th man.

26-MAN "PERFECT GAMES"

PITCHER	TEAM	DATE	"SPOILER"	OPP. TEAM
Hooks Wiltse	New York, NL	July 4, 1908	George McQuillan	Philadelphia
Tommy Bridges	Detroit, AL	Aug. 5, 1932	Dave Harris	Washington
Billy Pierce	Chicago, AL	June 28, 1958	Ed Fitz Gerald*	Washington
Milt Pappas	Cincinnati, NL	Sept. 2, 1972	Larry Stahl	San Diego
Milt Wilcox	Detroit, AL	April 15, 1983	Jerry Hairston	Chicago

*Extra base hit

WHO WAS THE ONLY PITCHER TO THROW A NO–HITTER ON HIS BIRTHDAY?

George M. Cohan, born on July 3, 1878, adopted the July 4 birthdate to become a, "Yankee Doodle Dandy." Louie Armstrong, raised in a foundling home, also adopted the July 4 birthdate, "'Cause it sounds patriotic," not knowing when his real birthdate was. And so, on this American day of days, when everyone else is throwing parades, it comes as no surprise that one pitcher, George Mullin of the Detroit Tigers, threw a birthday party of his own, by tossing a no–hitter on July 4, 1912, his 32nd birthday—the only major leaguer to give himself a no–hitter as a birthday present—and one of only three thrown on Independence Day, along with George Wiltse (1908) and Dave Righetti (1984).

WHO IS THE ONLY PITCHER OTHER THAN JOHNNY VANDER MEER TO THROW TWO NO–HIT GAMES WITHIN ONE CALENDAR MONTH?

When Johnny Vander Meer retired Leo Durocher for his 27th and final out on the night of June 16, 1938, he had not only thrown the first nighttime no–hitter in history, but had also stepped directly off the mound at Ebbets Field and into the pages of history, throwing two successive no–hitters. Before Vander Meer's second gem, only 10 pitchers had ever been credited with two no–hitters in their entire careers. None had ever thrown two in the same season, a feat that *The New York Times* trumpeted, "would never be duplicated." Since Vander Meer, a handful of pitchers have thrown two in a season, albeit none consecutively. Those who have thrown two no–hitters in one season are: Allie Reynolds, 1951; Virgil Trucks, 1952; Jim Maloney, 1965; and Nolan Ryan, 1973. The closest anyone came to duplicating Vander Meer's achievement came in 1947 when his then–teammate, the 6′6″ Ewell Blackwell, he of the famed Buggy Whip delivery which came from somewhere south of third, threw the second nighttime no–hitter in history. On June 18, against the same Boston Braves that Vander Meer had no–hit in the first of his masterpieces. Blackwell's next start came four days later against the Dodgers, the same team Vander Meer had pitched his second no–hitter against. And for eight and one-third innings, it looked like Blackwell would join Vander Meer in twin accomplishments. Then, facing the nearest thing to Durocher ever to take the field, Brooklyn shortstop Eddie Stanky, Blackwell forced him to hit a hard grounder back to the mound. It was so hard, in fact, that it went right between the legs of the rangy Blackwell, who failed by less than an inch to flag the ball down and preserve his no–hitter. But no matter, Blackwell's no–hitter was gone, and Vander Meer's name still stood alone as the only pitcher to pitch two consecutive no–hitters. And two in one month.

However, he finally got company, of sorts, in 1967, when Minnesota pitcher Dean Chance pitched a 2–1 no–hitter against the Cleveland Indians on August 25, his second no–hitter within a calendar month, his first having come 20 days earlier when, on August 5, he had pitched a five–inning, 2–0 perfect game against the Boston Red Sox.

WHO WAS THE ONLY PITCHER TO BOTH START AND FINISH EXACTLY 20 GAMES IN ONE SEASON?

History offers two explanations for the companionate claims that pitchers back in the so–called Good Old Days would always finish a game they started and not be relieved. One held that the pitching staffs were smaller and that the pitchers back then were stronger; hell, even their names, names like "Iron Man" Joe McGinnity, gave the lie to the slander that they could not finish games. The other claims that in today's era of specialization the relief pitcher has, like the contortionist, finally come into his own, and, starting with "Fireman" Johnny Murphy, the reliever has become an integral part of the game. Whatever the reason, few pitchers, like kids of the "I–say–it's–spinach–and––the–hell–with–it" school of eating, finish what's put before them. Gone are the days when a Jack Taylor would finish every game he started, as he did 33 times in both 1902 and 1903, following that feat with 39 starts and 39 complete games in 1904 and another 34 starts and the same number of complete games in 1905—a record total of 139 consecutive games started *and* finished. Gone, too, are the pitchers who pitch two games in one day, most unable to finish one a season. But in relatively recent times, one pitcher, Ted Lyons, did start and finish everything he set out to do: namely, starting and finishing exactly 20 games, a feat he performed in 1942, when, in 20 pitching appearances he logged a record of 14–6.

WHAT WAS THE ONLY YEAR BEFORE 1985 WHEN TWO MEN BECAME 300–GAME WINNERS?

When first Tom Seaver and then Phil Niekro each pitched their 300th win during the 1985 season, becoming, in order, the 17th and 18th members of this exclusive club, it became the second time in history that two men have passed the 300–game mark in one season. The first time came back in 1890 when pitchers Tim Keefe and Mickey Welch became the second and third men to join Pud Galvin as 300–game winners, a far more exclusive club than it has become 95 years later.

WHO WAS THE ONLY PITCHER TO HAVE TWO PERFECT SEASONS WITH AT LEAST FIVE DECISIONS?

The standard for a perfect season has always been Tom Zachary's 12–0 record for the 1929 New York Yankees. Not incidentally, Zachary also had a 2–0 season for the 1918 Philadelphia A's, when, pitching as "Zach Walton," he bivouacked on Connie Mack's doorstep while awaiting his call from the draft board to participate in the War to End all Wars. But when the Great Conflict was over, Walton returned home and ultimately signed up with the Washington Senators, where he would make history of another sort by delivering unto Babe Ruth the ball that Ruth swat for his 60th home run. However, even Tom Zachary–Zach Walton did not have two perfect seasons with at least five decisions. Only Wes Stock did, turning in a 5–0 record for the Baltimore Orioles in 1961 and then coming back with a 7–0 record in 1963. Unfortunately, Stock also had three years in which he registered no wins at all and was gone by 1967, taking with him his twin hills from which he could forever look down on those who followed him—two years in which he had perfect seasons with five or more decisions.

WHO IS THE ONLY MAN TO WIN 200 GAMES AND YET NOT HAVE A 20–GAME SEASON?

Contrary to popular belief, the best place to hide a needle is not in a haystack, but in amongst the other needles. The same holds true for trivia. Or for 200-game winners without a 20-game season for that matter. Now, it is normally thought that the two great benchmarks of pitching success, 20-game seasons and 200 wins, go hand-in-glove, one with the other. But it has been done. Those ancients who have committed themselves to a romantic and honorable devotion that holds that the inclusion of Federal League records is much like belching in church, would have you believe that there are two pitchers to win 200 games without benefit of a 20-game season, including in their total the name of John Pincus Quinn, who won either 247 games including the Federal League or 212 excluding the two-year league that stumbled through two inglorious years back in 1914 and 1915. And one of those Federal League years for Quinn was a 26-14 year, his only 20-game season. But the Federal League has been accepted by all authorities and must be accepted here. That leaves just one name: Milt Pappas, who won 209 games during his 17-year career, from 1957 to 1973, yet never was able to win more than 17 games in one season. However, before Pappas claims sole possession, it must be pointed out that Dodger pitcher Jerry Reuss has a total of 192 wins through 1985 with nary a 20-game season in sight, and with eight more wins joins Pappas as the second pitcher to win 200 games without a 20-game season.

Those other needles hidden amongst the 20-game and 200-game winners include six pitchers who had at least two 20-game seasons and yet not have a winning career record (Jack Powell, 1902 and '05; Bill Dineen, 1902, '03 and '04; Jim Scott, 1913 and '15; Bobo Newsom, 1938, '39 and '40; Bill Singer, 1969 and '73; and Randy Jones, 1975 and '76) and the three pitchers who pitched at least 20 years, past the age when any self-respecting pitcher would have been home in bed, and had neither a 20-game season nor 200 wins: Lindy McDaniel, Curt Simmons and Hoyt Wilhelm.

4th Inning
The Hall of Fame

WHAT THREE HALL OF FAME PITCHERS WERE ON THE LOSING ENDS OF PERFECT GAMES THROWN BY OTHER HALL OF FAME PITCHERS?

The Perfect Game is one of baseball's rarest achievements, rivaling the poker player's pulling to an inside royal straight flush and filling it. Since the beginning of time—and baseball as well—there have been but 13 Perfect Games and three times Hall of Fame pitchers were on the losing end of one of those classics thrown by yet another member of the Hall of Fame. That Hall of Fame trio with *brio* follows: Pud Galvin, who was the losing pitcher when Montgomery Ward threw his Perfect Game on June 17, 1880; Rube Waddell, who lost to Cy Young when Young threw his Perfect Game on May 5, 1904; and Ed Walsh, who lost on a wild pitch when Addie Joss pitched his Perfect Game on October 2, 1908.

NAME THE FOUR MEMBERS OF THE HALL OF FAME WHOSE MANAGERIAL WON–LOST PERCENTAGE WAS LOWER THAN THEIR LIFETIME BATTING AVERAGE.

Cooperstown is at once a patch of ground and a state of emotion. Its Hall of Fame is inhabited by 158 baseball monuments erected in tribute to on-the-field genius. But when these baseball greats tried their hands at managing, the gilt of their greatness sometimes peeled off for all to see. Four of them even managed to wind up with lower won–lost records than their lifetime batting averages—no mean feat when you consider that Connie Mack, baseball's all–time losingest manager, had a won–lost percentage of .484. Those four great players, but less–than–great managers, were as follows: Luke Appling, lifetime batting average .310, managerial won–lost record 10-30, percentage .250; Jim Bottomley, lifetime batting average .310, managerial won–lost record 21-58, percentage .266; Roger Connor, lifetime batting average .318, managerial won–lost record 9-37, percentage .196; and Honus Wagner, lifetime batting average .329, managerial won–lost record 1-4, percentage .200.

WHAT FUTURE HALL OF FAME PITCHER HAD A COMPLETE GAME IN HIS ROOKIE YEAR AND YET FINISHED WITH AN 0–0 RECORD?

Sometimes baseball writers will attempt to explain the unknowable in terms not worth knowing. Most times those incidents occur when they come up against baseball's rules. Those rules, originally handed down from baseball's mount by Alexander Cartwright and amended less times than the U.S. Constitution, are engraved in stone and cover almost every exigency. One such rule is the "Forfeit" rule, Rule 24, which holds that, "In a regulation game which the umpire shall declare forfeited after four–and–a–half innings have been played, all individual and team averages shall be incorporated in the official playing records, except that no pitcher shall be credited with a victory or charged with a loss in said game." The rule was invoked on September 26, 1942 when, with rookie Warren Spahn on the mound for the Boston Braves against the New York Giants and losing 5–2 in the eighth inning, a horde of kids, who had been let in free as part of a wartime scrap metal drive, descended onto the field. Unable to clear the kids off the field, the umpires declared the game "Forfeit," the Braves winning 9–0 and all the records—except the allocation of a win or loss for the pitcher—left standing. Thus, Spahn, who has credit for one complete game in his first year in the majors, escaped without a loss, explaining what appears to be an obvious misprint in the *MacMillan Baseball Encyclopedia*. But then again, baseball's "Bible" is no different from any other Bible, misleading at a cursory glance—like having your daughter come home at four in the morning with the Gideon Bible tucked under her arm. There is an explanation for everything, even Spahn's 0–0 record with one complete game to his credit in 1942.

WHAT WAS THE ONLY TRADE IN WHICH THREE FUTURE HALL OF FAMERS WERE INVOLVED?

Throughout history there have been trades. And then there have been trades. And some of those have been, not to coin a phrase, "beauts." Managers have been traded for each other (as in Dykes for Gordon), coaches have been traded for each other (as in Appling for Jo–Jo White), players have been traded for themselves (as in Harry Chiti for "a player to be named later," who turned out to be Harry Chiti), and even wives have been traded (as in Petersen and Kekich's, "life swap not a wife swap").

The minor leagues have also had their share of unusual trades. Pitcher Joe Martina was once acquired by the New Orleans Pelicans of the Southern Association for a sack of oysters. And first baseman Jack Fenton was acquired by the San Francisco Seals of the Pacific Coast League for a carton of prunes. But perhaps the most classic of trades was the one engineered by Joe Engel, "The Barnum of the Bushes," president of the Chattanooga Lookouts, when he traded shortstop Johnny Jones to Charlotte in the Sally League for a 25–pound turkey. Inviting some 25 sportswriters to a dinner where he promised to taste, "the new meat on his team", Engel, afterwards, was forced to admit, "I think I got the worst of that deal. That was a mighty tough turkey."

Getting the worst of a deal has always haunted management types, many of whom claim, "The best trades are the ones that aren't made." But one that was made came in 1916, when John McGraw, using his well–stocked roster like trading cards, starting wheeling and dealing to build his Giants into a pennant contender. On July 20th he was to send pitcher Christy Mathewson to Cincinnati where he would take over as manager, together with infielder Bill McKechnie, and outfielder Edd Rousch for outfielder Red Killefer and infielder Buck Herzog. Not only did the deal work—for both teams—New York winning the pennant in 1917 and Cincinnati in 1919, but all three men sent apacking to Cincinnati would later become members of the Hall of Fame, the only time three future Hall of Famers were involved in one trade.

WHAT HALL OF FAMER IS THE CO–HOLDER OF THE RECORD FOR MOST ERRORS AT HIS POSITION FOR ONE GAME?

It is more than ironic that the only plaque in the Hall of Fame which carries the adjective "graceful" belongs to Napoleon Lajoie, who in his salad days had been as light as a cucumber sandwich in his moves on the field. For years his handiwork around second base for the Cleveland Indians had been less that of the occasional heroics sportswriters feed upon than those appreciated by dues–paying fans as he approached even ordinary games with out–of–the–ordinary performances. Four times Lajoie would lead the American League in putouts, six times in fielding average, three times in assists, three times in double plays, and six times in total fielding chances per game. In short, Lajoie spreadeagled the field—and second base as well. But by the twilight of his career, his moves were those of a man who moved as if drugged by the scent of a reconstituted past. And so it was that in his twentieth year he was shipped off to one of the most woeful teams of all time, the 1915 Philadelphia A's. There Lajoie somehow managed to manhandle five balls hit in his direction on the afternoon of April 22, 1915, tying the all–time record for most miscues with Piano Legs Hickman, a man who had played with him at Cleveland and who occasionally had spelled him at second base.

WHO IS THE ONLY PITCHER IN THE HALL OF FAME WITH A LOSING RECORD?

No less than 50 players have been elected to the Hall of Fame on the basis of their achievements as pitchers. But, despite that sparsely populated island of greatness that these half–a–hundred occupy, one of them is honored for his contributions over and above his won–lost record which shows a negative balance. Discounting Candy Cummings, whose won–lost record in National League play shows him with 21 wins and 22 losses in two seasons, but who had a record of 194 wins and 129 losses in his four years in the earlier National Association (between 1872 and 1875), the only pitcher in the Hall of Fame with a deficit record is Satchel Paige, who was elected in 1971 "on the basis of his career in the Negro Leagues" rather than his 28–31 record in the major leagues.

However, there are many who believe that if for nothing else, Leroy "Satchel" Paige should be enshrined in the Hall of Fame for his six rules on "How to Stay Young."

Avoid fried meats which angry up the blood.

If your stomach disputes you, lie down and pacify it with cool thoughts.

Keep the juices flowing by jangling around gently as you move.

Go very light on the vices, such as carrying on in society, the social ramble ain't restful.

Avoid running at all times.

Don't look back. Something might be gaining on you.

WHAT TWO HALL OF FAMERS INVENTED ANOTHER SPORT?

Only if you're the "Curious George" type and leafing through a book to find curiosities other than baseball trivia would your eye spot the following item in Frank G. Menke's *Encyclopedia of Sports* under Bowling: "In the spring of 1900, Wilbert Robinson and John J. McGraw, both baseball immortals and then co–owners of the Diamond Bowling Alleys in Baltimore, Md., introduced the game known as duck pins. Frank Van Sant, their alley manager, suggested a set of tenpins be converted into little pins to conform with the six–inch bowling ball which was used in the games of five–back and cocked hat. John Ditmar, a Baltimore woodturner, produced the first set of duck pins.

"When Robinson and McGraw, whose hobby was shooting ducks, saw the little pins fly and scatter all over the place, they remarked that they looked like a flock of flying ducks. Bill Clarke, a sportswriter on the Baltimore *Morning Sun,* in his story the following day, christened them duck pins, and the name stuck."

WHAT MODERN HALL OF FAME PITCHER HAD THE HIGHEST AVERAGE NUMBER OF WINS PER SEASON PITCHED?

The turn of the century was a celebration for America, cocksure now of her future, but searching for some way to identify herself to the world as an emerging great nation. The baseball scene also was populated by tintypes who wore nicknames which allowed the world to identify them with their place of origin, their skills, or even their dispositions. Crowded in amongst Little Napoleon (McGraw), Happy Jack (Chesbro), and The Amateur (Breitenstein) were some appellations that were even more fanciful, such as Bob Ferguson's colorful nickname, Death to Flying Things, or Pud Galvin's The Little Steam Engine.

But of all the nicknames, the most utilitarian was the one hung on Joseph Jerome McGinnity, "Iron Man." The name was derived from a comment by McGinnity, himself, who, when he originally signed with Baltimore of the old National League, was asked what he did. "I'm an iron man," McGinnity replied. And Iron Man he was, winning 247 games over a 10–year span, an average of 24.7 per season pitched and the highest average in the Hall of Fame, nosing out Kid Nichols' average of 24.0 wins per year. But it wasn't merely his wins nor the average number of wins per year that made McGinnity an Iron Man. McGinnity earned the title the hard way. Throwing his famous submarine pitch, "Old Sal" McGinnity, who could no more be rattled than ice welded or iron melted, three times in the month of August, 1903, took the mound in both ends of a double header, and three times pitched and won two complete games in one day. The only pitcher ever to win 25 or more games with three different teams (Baltimore, Brooklyn, and New York), McGinnity is one of the four pitchers enshrined in the Hall of Fame who never had a losing season. The other three are Dizzy Dean, Addie Joss, and A.G. Spalding. And he is also the Hall of Fame pitcher with the highest average number of wins per season pitched.

WHAT TWO HALL OF FAME PITCHERS MADE THEIR LAST MAJOR LEAGUE APPEARANCE AGAINST EACH OTHER?

Just as they had many times before, including the memorable 1908 Play–Off game occasioned by Merkle's failure to touch second, Christy Mathewson and Mordecai Centennial "Three Finger" Brown met once again by prearrangement on September 4, 1916 to do battle. Mathewson, by now the manager of the Cincinnati Reds, had come over in a trade only that July from the Giants where he had won 372 games and felt that, his pitching career over, he would like to embark upon yet another career, that of managing. But the old urge to pitch again, to hear the echoes of an earlier day, moved him and he agreed to pitch the second game of a Labor Day double-header in Chicago. His opponent was the legendary "Three Finger" Brown, also ending his long and legendary career with the Cubs. With both pitchers pitching from memory, their divine spark of fire gone, the game was nothing like the classic match-ups for which they had become famous. Mathewson would stagger through, allowing 14 hits and eight runs. But Brown's performance was worse, if that's possible, as he allowed a total of 18 hits and 10 runs. The final score was 10–8, Mathewson, the same as their lifetime pitching records against each other. This final meeting marked the last appearance on the mound for both—and the only time Mathewson would pitch in a uniform other than that of his beloved New York Giants.

WHAT HALL OF FAMER PLAYED THE MOST GAMES, ALL AT ONE POSITION?

Some of those enshrined in the Hall of Fame played every position available to them, like Cap Anson and Roger Bresnahan, who both played all nine positions during their storied careers. Others have specialized and have become identified with one position and have been rewarded because of their expertise in and around that position. Brooks Robinson is one who played more games at third than any other player, 2,870. But Robinson also put in an assorted 33 games at other infield positions. Willie Mays played the most at *one* position, centerfield, 2,038, but also filled in for 38 games at first and sundry other positions. Only one nonpitcher in the Hall of Fame stayed put his entire career at one position: Luis Aparicio, who played shortstop and nothing but shortstop for his entire 2,581–game career, the Hall of Famer who played the most games *all* at one position.

WHAT THREE HALL OF FAMERS DIED ON THEIR BIRTHDAYS?

Psychological studies have shown that most people do not perish on the day before their birthday or on Christmas or on New Years, but, instead, have the will to live to make that special day. Three Hall of Famers who were called by that Great Umpire in the Sky on that special day, their birthday, were: Joe Tinker, on July 27 (1880–1948); Gabby Hartnett, on December 20 (1900–1972); and Bucky Harris, on November 8 (1896–1977).

5th Inning
The World Series

WHO HOLDS THE RECORD FOR HITTING SAFELY IN THE MOST CONSECUTIVE WORLD SERIES GAMES?

Not unlike bingo halls, which have the rule that "Winners must be present," those who set World Series records have first to be present before they're accounted for. One of those who seemed always to be present was Hank Bauer, who played in 53 World Series games, the fourth greatest number in World Series history behind fellow Yankees Yogi Berra, Mickey Mantle, and Elston Howard. Held hitless in the last game of the 1955 World Series by Johnny Podres of the Dodgers, Bauer started his consecutive hit streak in the first game of the 1956 World Series against Sal Maglie, going two–for–five. Throughout the rest of the 1956 and 1957 Classics, Bauer connected in each of the seven games and continued for the first three games of the 1958 World Series—including stroking a homer in each of those first three games, a World Series record for homers in consecutive games—until Warren Spahn blanked him in the fourth game, a total of 17 consecutive games. The National League record is held by Roberto Clemente, who had at least one hit in each of the 14 World Series games in the only two World Series he ever played in, 1960 and 1971.

WHAT FOUR MEN WERE ON THE MOST LOSING WORLD SERIES TEAMS?

According to the *MacMillan Baseball Encyclopedia,* both Harold "Pee Wee" Reese and Elston Howard played for six World Series losers. Reese, who played in all 44 World Series games between the Brooklyn Dodgers and the New York Yankees, was on the losing side in every World Series but one—losing to the Yankees in 1941, 1947, 1949, 1952, 1953, and 1956 and winning only in 1955. Howard was on the winning side in 1956, 1958, 1961, and 1962 as a member of the New York Yankees and on the losing side in 1955, 1957, 1960, 1963, and 1964 as a Yankee and in 1967 playing with the Boston Red Sox. The third man is John McGraw, the second winningest manager of all time, but the loser of six of his nine World Series appearances; his New York Giants lost in 1911, 1912, 1913, 1917, 1923, and 1924. And the fourth? To find him you'll need both the *Encyclopedia* and the official team rosters. He's Fred Merkle, who suffered along with McGraw in 1911, 1912, and 1913, then lost with Brooklyn in 1916 and the Chicago Cubs in 1918 and, in his last year, was on the roster and eligible to play, but didn't, in the 1926 World Series for the Yankees in their losing effort that fall, his sixth losing World Series team.

WHO IS THE ONLY PITCHER TO WIN WORLD SERIES GAMES IN THREE DIFFERENT DECADES?

Those pitchers who have won three or more games in the World Series dot its magnificent landscape like Christmas tree lights, their feats shining for all to see. But of all the pitchers who have won three or more games, only one, Jim Palmer of the Baltimore Orioles, ever turned this epic feat of arms in three different decades: the 1960s the 1970s and the 1980s. From the time he arrived on the scene in 1965, Jim Palmer carried a flame of greatness, his pitching radiating a hard glow of high purpose. Pitted against Sandy Koufax in what would be the great left–hander's last appearance in the Majors, the then 20–year–old Palmer outdueled the old master in the second game of the 1966 World Series, thus becoming the youngest pitcher ever to throw a World Series shutout. By 1970 his fastball and curve working to perfection, he had Cincinnati batters weaving castles in the air with their bats, a feat he repeated with yet another win in 1971 against the Pirates. And then 12 years later, Palmer, reduced by now to relief status, his once brilliant fires that had flamed into being at his every command in his earlier day now but a flicker, came on in relief of Oriole starter Mike Flanagan the third game of the 1983 World Series to hold the Phillies scoreless for two innings and pick up the win, his last win in the Major Leagues, and the win that would make him the only pitcher ever to win World Series games in three different decades.

WHO HAS THE HIGHEST WORLD SERIES BATTING AVERAGE FOR ANY PLAYER WHO PLAYED 20 OR MORE YEARS IN THE MAJORS?

Many of those who played 20 years in the majors never made it to the World Series, greats like Luke Appling and Nap Lajoie and near-greats like Mickey Vernon and Bill Dahlen. But one who did and had the highest lifetime World Series batting average of any of the Geritol Set who had been around 20 or more years to show for it was Maximilian Carnarius, known as Max Carey for short, but not for long in World Series play. He played only in the 1925 Series for the come–from–behind Pittsburgh Pirates who won the last three games of the Series to beat Walter Johnson and the Washington Senators, four games to three. In that Series, his only one, Carey had 11 hits in 24 at–bats for an average of .458 for one Series. And, not incidentally, for his entire 20–year–career, the highest lifetime World Series batting average for any player who played 20 or more years.

WHO WAS THE ONLY PLAYER TO END A SERIES BY TAKING A CALLED THIRD STRIKE?

Back in the early days of baseball, somewhere between the Paleozoic and the modern era, there was a singing umpire named William Byron, or "Lord Byron," as he was called, who, in his heyday would greet every batter who took a called third strike with a little ditty that went, "You can't get a hit with a bat on your shoulder . . . da, da, da, dum. . . ."

But it wasn't Byron but William "Barry" McCormick who stood behind the plate for the seventh and final game of the 1925 World Series between the Pittsburgh Pirates and Washington Senators and called Washington slugger Goose Goslin "Out" on a called third strike delivered by Pirate pitcher Red Oldham to end one of the greatest World Series up to that time in history. The Pirates had come back from a 1–3 deficit to beat the Senators and their great pitcher Walter Johnson. Other batters have ended the World Series by striking out, but all of them struck out swinging—Wagner in 1903, Kuhel in 1933, Chartak in 1944, Hodges in 1949, Lopata in 1950, Robinson in 1956, Allison in 1965, Scott in 1967, Wilson in 1980, and Thomas in 1982—leaving Goslin with the dubious distinction of posing with the bat on his shoulder when the World Series ended for his team.

Ironically, Goslin—who also had the distinction of being the only Washington Senator to play in all 19 games the Senators ever played in the World Series and the co-holder for the most consecutive hits in a World Series, six in 1924—would end another Series: the 1935 World Series when his single in the bottom of the ninth scored Mickey Cochrane with the run that enabled Detroit to win its first World Series, beating the Cubs in six games.

WHO WAS THE ONLY PITCHER TO APPEAR IN ALL SEVEN GAMES OF A SEVEN-GAME WORLD SERIES?

As long as the World Series continues with its present seven–game format, something that was reinstated in 1922, the way God and Judge Landis intended it to be, this is one of those baseball records that is guaranteed never to be broken, along with the record held by Pete Gray and One–Arm Daly, there being no chance of a man with no arms playing in the majors. The man who is already enshrined in the Baseball Hall of Trivia, never to be dislodged, is Darold Knowles, the relief pitcher for the Oakland A's, who pitched in all seven games of the 1973 Series, albeit for a total of only six–plus innings. Viewed by his opposition, the New York Mets, with the same amount of affection Europeans had once lavished on the hordes of invading Huns, Knowles performed in much the same efficient manner. He gave up only four hits and no earned runs in the six and one-third innings he pitched, and picked up two vital saves, wrapping up his personal "scorched earth" campaign by coming in to retire the last man to come to bat in the World Series, Wayne Garrett, on a harmless pop–up to short.

WHO ARE THE ONLY TWO PLAYERS TO PLAY IN THE WORLD SERIES FOR THE SAME MANAGER IN BOTH LEAGUES?

Let your fingers do the walking, running, and sliding through the *MacMillan Baseball Encyclopedia* and you'll find several players who have played for World Series teams in both leagues, starting with Jimmy Archer, who caught for the 1907 Detroit Tigers and the 1910 Chicago Cubs. But only two of those who have appeared in the World Series for clubs in both leagues have played under the same manager—Pat Malone and Milt Wilcox. Malone pitched for Joe McCarthy's 1929 Chicago Cubs team and then followed McCarthy to the New York Yankees—after first facing him in the 1932 World Series—where he appeared in the 1936 World Series. Wilcox pitched for Sparky Anderson's 1970 Cincinnati Reds and then became a part of Anderson's 1984 Detroit Tigers. Not only were the two pitchers following their old mentors, but each bettered himself in his second association, going from Series loser to Series winner.

NAME THE FOUR ROOKIES WHO HAVE STARTED—AND WON—THE FIRST GAME OF A WORLD SERIES.

In the 77 World Series played through 1985, over 125 pitchers pitching in their first full season in the major leagues have been brought in to pitch, but only four rookies have ever started *and* won the opening game of a Series: Babe Adams in 1909, Spec Shea in 1947, Joe Black in 1952, and Bob Walk in 1980. No less than 33 rookies have started games in the Series and 16 have won their games. But only six have ever been tapped to pitch the opening game—Babe Adams in 1909 for the Pirates, Paul Derringer in 1931 for the Cardinals, Spec Shea in 1947 for the Yankees, Don Newcombe in 1949 for the Dodgers, Joe Black in 1952 for the Dodgers, and Bob Walk in 1980 for the Phillies. And only Adams, Shea, Black and Walk won their postseason debuts, with Adams winning three times in the 1909 Series, Shea twice in 1947, Black once while losing twice in 1952, and Walk once in 1980.

NAME THE ONLY SIX BLACK PITCHERS EVER TO WIN A WORLD SERIES GAME.

Dating back to the fifth game of the 1948 World Series, when Satchel Paige and his "hesitation" pitch made a brief two–thirds of an inning appearance for the Cleveland Indians against the Boston Braves, a total of 20 black pitchers have pitched in the Series. But only six have wins to show for their efforts. And one of them, Bob Gibson of the St. Louis Cardinals, holds several World Series records, including most games won in a row, with seven, and most strikeouts, with 17.

The other five who have won World Series games are Joe

Black, who won the first game of the 1952 Series for Brooklyn; Jim "Mudcat" Grant, who won the first and sixth games of the 1965 Series for the Twins; John Wyatt, who won the sixth game of the 1967 Series for the Red Sox in relief; Blue Moon Odom, who won the fifth and final game of the 1974 Series for the Oakland A's; and Grant Jackson, who won the final game of the 1979 Series in relief for the Pirates.

WHAT PLAYER'S FIRST AND LAST WORLD SERIES APPEARANCES WERE THE MOST YEARS APART?

Several great and near–greats have used the World Series as their own form of gentrification, refusing to surrender to the undeniable facts of advancing age. The books are filled with the exploits of Grover Cleveland Alexander, "Old Pete" as he was called by the sportswriters who chronicled his heroics, pitching through his own personal fogbanks to strike out Tony Lazzeri in the 1926 World Series, 11 years after his first fall classic. And of Babe Ruth—the sands in his personal hourglass of greatness sifting down, pointing somewhere in the vague direction of Wrigley Field's fence. Or was his beau gesture merely gesticulating unspeakable acts in the direction of the opposing pitcher and acquitting himself by parking the ball in the bleachers on the next pitch in the 1932 Series, a full 17 years after his first appearance. Others who have spanned the years include Rabbit Maranville, who, 14 years after going 4–for–13 in the 1914 World Series again went 4–for–13 in the 1928 Series; Jim Kaat, who relieved in four games in the 1982 World Series, 17 years after first appearing in a Series; Babe Adams and Stuffy McInnis, both of whom appeared in the 1925 World Series 16 and 15 years after their first appearances; and Herb Pennock, whose World Series career spanned 18 years, his first appearance coming in 1915, his last in 1932.

But the player who spanned the most time between his first and last appearance was Willie Mays, who first played in the Series in 1951 as the "Say Hey" kid, full of cannonade and vinegar, and ended his career 22 years later as a member of the '73 New York Mets looking less like a baseball figure than a father figure. But to New York fans, who had come to view Willie as their municipal monument, it made no never mind; his very presence on the field was a magic memory even if it was merely a memory of his once greatness now enshrined with the mortgage of age.

NAME THE ONLY FOUR MAJOR LEAGUERS TO HAVE HAD THE SAME LIFETIME BATTING AVERAGE AS THEIR WORLD SERIES BATTING AVERAGE.

Consistency might be the hobgoblin of little minds, but in baseball trivia it is an asset devoutly to be desired. The careers of too many players are dimmed by the dazzling inconsistency of their performance. Perhaps the ultimate in consistency is the ability to deliver exactly what is asked of one, no more nor less. And four players did this in World Series play, having exactly the same batting average for their entire World Series career as they had during their lifetimes in the majors.

Those four models of consistency are: Danny Murphy, who in 16 years, from 1900 through 1915, hit .288, the same as he did in three World Series; Duffy Lewis, who in 11 years, from 1910 through 1921, hit .284, the same as he did in three Series; Paul Waner, who in 20 years, from 1926 through 1945, hit .333, the same as he did in his one World Series appearance; and Phil Linz who in seven years, from 1962 through 1968, hit .235, the same as he did in his two World Series, completing the short list of those who had the same lifetime batting averages in both regular season and World Series play.

WHAT WAS THE FIRST WORLD SERIES GAME EVER BROADCAST?

Radio came bursting onto the scene in the early 1920s, a revolutionary instrument to some and a conduit through which prefabricated din could be funneled into living rooms for others. But whatever it was, it wasn't long before it found baseball, or vice versa, with the first broadcast of a baseball game beaming from KDKA, Pittsburgh, back on the afternoon of August 5, 1921, when broadcaster Harold Arlin told a breathlessly waiting world—at least that portion of it near the Monongahela River—the outcome of a game between the second–place Pirates and the last–place Phillies. That very same year, 1921, the first quasi–broadcast of a World Series game took place, with sportswriter Grantland Rice calling the local WJZ studios from the pressbox to pass along the goings–on at the Polo Grounds between the Giants and the Yankees for rebroadcast over the airwaves by studio announcer Tommy Cowan. But the very first Series to be broadcast live was the 1922 Series between the Giants and the Yankees with Grantland Rice doing the play–by–play direct from the Polo Grounds. By 1923 the broadcast of the Series had become a tradition, even if it were only a two–year tradition. And for the 1923 Series, the NBC flagship station, WJZ, had hired radio announcer Graham McNamee, he of the bell–shaped tones. It was a case of permitting a speaker to describe without fear of contradiction, as McNamee wove word pictures all afternoon long, never letting the facts on the field interfere with his narrative. After the first game of the 1923 Series, writer Ring Lardner, who had been seated next to

McNamee all afternoon, got up and said to everyone in general, "They must have been playing a doubleheader here this afternoon—the game I saw and the game McNamee announced." That too would be the beginning of a tradition.

WHO WAS THE ONLY PLAYER IN WORLD SERIES HISTORY TO HIT TWO HOME RUNS IN HIS FIRST TWO TIMES AT BAT?

Several players have hit home runs their first time up in World Series competition—including pitcher Mickey Lolich, who hit his one and only Major League home run his first time up in the 1968 Series, and Jim Mason of the Yankees who hit one in his only time up in the Series. But only Gene Tenace, Oakland A's catcher and utility jack–of–all trades, hit two his first two times at bat, duplicating Bob Nieman's famous feat of hitting two in his first two times up in the Majors.

Playing in place of the injured Dave Duncan, Tenace—who had only five homers in regular season play—drove in nine runs and tied the World Series record for a seven game Series with four homers in the 1972 classic. Two of them were in his first two times up. This candidate for the "Unlikeliest World Series Hero" list also made Series history by being the first player with a hairpiece to play in the World Series.

WHAT PITCHER HAS THE MOST HITS IN WORLD SERIES PLAY?

With the designated hitter rule in vogue in World Series play since 1973, pitchers have had little or no chance of showcasing their hitting talents. Or, as the case more often is, their lack of hitting talents. A case in point is George Earnshaw's inverse record of 0–22 in Series play. Tim Stoddard is the last pitcher to get a hit in Series play and that came in his only official appearance back in 19–aught–79. Since then, even when pitchers come to the plate in every odd year, they normally use their bat to air-condition the premises rather than to make contact with the ball, their performances at the plate about as exciting as watching a tree form its annual ring. However, back when a pitcher's existence was defined by the four walls of a stadium, not merely the pitcher's mound, pitchers were expected to contribute to their team's offense. One who did, quite handily, thank you, was Christy Mathewson, he of the famous "Fadeaway Pitch" and three shutout wins in the 1905 World Series. Mathewson came to bat no less than 32 times in four different Series, and managed to get nine hits, the most for any pitcher in World Series history. Matty's nine hits are one more than Jack Coombs had in three Series and Allie Reynolds in six Series, a record which, thanks to the designated hitter rule, appears to be in no jeopardy whatsoever of being surpassed.

WHO IS THE ONLY PITCHER TO WIN MORE GAMES IN THE WORLD SERIES THAN HE HAD DURING THE REGULAR SEASON?

With the end of World War II, Johnny came marching home again—along with Teddy and Hank and just about everybody else who had once been part of major league baseball—joining teams as fast as they could be mustered out of the military. Baseball waived its traditional rule that only those players who had been on the rosters on September 1 were eligible to play in the World Series that year, providing in one swell foop two of the most interesting members of the Trivia Hall of Fame.

One of the returning Cubbies that year was Clyde McCullough, who had come back too late to participate in regular season play, but was allowed to play in the 1945 Series. McCullough came to bat once as a pinch–hitter—striking out in the bottom of the ninth in the final game—thereby becoming the only player in Series history to appear in the Series without playing a game during the regular season.

And along with McCullough came a returning fireman, or more accurately, Virgil "Fireman" Trucks, the pitcher for the Detroit Tigers who had just spent two years in the employ of the United States Navy. Trucks managed to sneak in a little practice with the Tigers, appearing in all of one game, pitching for a total of five and one–third innings. During the '45 Series, Tiger manager Steve O'Neill made use of Trucks, starting him in the second game. Trucks rewarded O'Neill and the Tigers by winning the second game with a seven–hit 4–1 complete–game win—the only pitcher to win more games in the World Series than he had during the regular season.

Two other pitchers have equaled their entire season win total in World Series competition to run Trucks a close second: Paul Lindblad in the 1973 Series for Oakland and "Blue Moon" Odom in the 1974 Series for the same Oakland A's, both 1–0 as relievers despite season records of 1–4 and 1–5 respectively.

WHO WAS THE ONLY PITCHER TO HIT A WORLD SERIES HOME RUN IN A LOSING CAUSE?

World Series history was made on October 10, 1920, when Jim Bagby became the first pitcher to hit a Series home run. Not incidentally, Bagby was also the winning pitcher that afternoon as the Indians beat the Dodgers 8–1. Unfortunately, Bagby's achievement was overshadowed by the equally singular feats of two teamates: Elmer Smith's grand slam homer, the first in Series history; and Bill Wambsganss' unassisted triple play, the first, and only, such play in Series history. And so it has gone throughout the subsequent 65 World Series—those 12 pitchers who have hit homers usually hitting them in support of their own winning efforts and just as usually having them overshadowed by some other batter's accomplishment(s). Oh sure, occasionally their home run heroics will be remembered, as when Bucky Walter's bat provided him with all the runs he needed in the sixth game of the 1940 Series or when Dave McNally hit a grand slammer in his own cause to outscore the Reds team in the third game of the '70 Series. But more often than not the pitcher's round-tripper merely gets shuffled into his total performance for the day, overlooked in his winning effort. However, twice the pitcher hitting the homer has *not* been the winning pitcher. It happened to the above mentioned McNally in the fifth game of the 1969 World Series when the Oriole hurler, pitching in the decisive fifth game against the Mets, hit a two-run homer and yet was not around for the the end of the game, the loss going to Eddie Watt in relief. But even so, McNally got away better than did Jose Santiago, the only man to hit a World Series home run in a losing cause. Santiago, pitching the opening game of the 1967 Series, gave the Red Sox all of their runs in a 2–1 loss to the Cardinals and Bob Gibson—the same Bob Gibson who would personally come back to homer in the seventh game behind his third Series win, one of two homers Gibson had in Series competition, tying McNally for most Series homers by a pitcher.

WHAT WAS THE ONLY GAME IN WORLD SERIES HISTORY IN WHICH FOUR MEN GOT FOUR HITS?

The 1946 World Series between the St. Louis Cardinals and the Boston Red Sox will be remembered from that time and forevermore for one play and one play alone: the dash to daylight by Enos Slaughter in the seventh game, a bit of base running derring–do that had to be seen to be disbelieved. After all this time, the mind retains the essentials and rejects superficialties. And the essentials were that the Red Sox had just tied the score 3–3 in the top of the eighth with two runs on a double by Dom DiMaggio. But DiMaggio, running out the double, had twisted his ankle and had to be replaced by pinch runner Leon Culberson. When St. Louis came to bat in its half of the eighth, Culberson took DiMaggio's place in center field as well. And Boston manager Joe Cronin, having pinch hit for pitcher Joe Dobson, went to the bullpen, calling in right–hander Bob Klinger. The first man to face Klinger was the left–handed Enos "Country" Slaughter, who inhospitably welcomed Klinger with a single. But Slaughter was to languish on first as the next two batters, Whitey Kurowski and Del Rice, went down. The next batter up was left–handed Harry "The Hat" Walker. And St. Louis manager Eddie Dyer, trying to make something, anything, happen, signaled for the hit–and–run. As Klinger came down with the pitch, Slaughter, who was poised on first like a dog that sees a pheasant, lit out for second. As Walker made contact with the ball, driving it into the gap in centerfield, Slaughter continued his way around second, head down, heading ball's-out for third. Culberson, slightly slower than DiMaggio, was in the process of chasing the ball down, and fumbled it momentarily as Slaughter neared third. Without slowing up, and despite third base coach Mike Gonzalez's outstretched hands signaling for him to hold at third, Slaughter continued on his mad tear around third, under his own instructions. Boston shortstop Johnny Pesky, seeing Gonzalez's upraised hands and fully expecting Slaughter to stop at third, got the relay from Culberson in short left field, taking it over his left shoulder and then, turning slowly, he realized the urgency of the situation—an urgency that Slaughter was impressing upon Pesky and all of those in Sportsman's Park, as he continued to roar toward home, taking about as much time to do so as it takes to roar "Here I come." Only then did Pesky grasp the situation and fire the ball home to Boston catcher Roy Partee. But too late. Slaughter had slid in around Partee's wide tag with the fourth and winning run—the run that would give the Cardinals the Series by the same 4–3 margin.

But what few remember about that same Series was that the fourth game produced the greatest number of hit records in Series history. For not only did the Cardinals get 20 hits in that game, tying a 25–year–old record for most hits in one Series game by the 1921 New York Giants, but four men tied a then—Series record as well, all getting four hits. The four men—all of whom tied the one-game hit record originally set by Pirate third baseman Tommy Leach in the very first World Series game ever, October 1, 1903—were Slaughter, Whitey Kurowski, and Joe Gariagola of the Cards and Wally Moses of the Red Sox. They thus became the 23rd, 24th, 25th and 26th men to get four hits in one Series game, that order, by all getting singles in the ninth. And although the record was ultimately eclipsed by Paul Molitar, who got five hits in the first game of the '82 Series, these four batsmen represented the most prolific one-game outburst in World Series history.

WHO WAS THE OLDEST PITCHER EVER TO PITCH A COMPLETE GAME IN THE WORLD SERIES?

The year was 1926 and the St. Louis Cardinals, perennial also-rans, were also running. They were in fourth place and in desperate need of pitching help. In that year they got it, claiming aging Grover Cleveland Alexander from the Chicago Cubs for the $4,000 waiver price.

The Great Alex had been around for 15 years, winning 328

games—including eight 20–game seasons and three 30–game seasons. However, his reputation was not based on his pitching prowess alone. Alexander was equally adept at the bottle and seemed always to be wandering off in search of a place dispensing lawful—or in those days of Prohibition—unlawful cheer. It was felt by most that Alex's greatness was behind him; that he was dissipated, drank too much, and because he had broken his ankle in spring training that year, was through as a big league pitcher at the age of 39.

But it wasn't his dissipation, drunkenness, or disability that finished him with the Cubs. It was what Cub manager Joe McCarthy viewed as his insubordination. On the occasion in question, McCarthy was running down the strengths and weaknesses of the opposing batters on the Dodgers, telling Alexander how to pitch to each. When the name Rabbit Maranville—the man they called, "The Ancient Mariner," because he, "stoppeth only one in three," and who had been with the Cubs only the previous year—came up, McCarthy said, "We'll have to switch signs whenever he gets on second base. He's smart enough to remember our signs from last year." Alex, tiring of the sermon, remarked snidely, "Well, now, if we thought there was much chance of this guy gettin' on second base, we wouldn't have got rid of him, would we?"

By the time the Cubs had moved to Philadelphia, Alexander's remark had earned him a place on the waiver list, tossed onto baseball's scrap heap like an antique without worth, there to be picked up by the Cardinals.

Cardinal manager Rogers Hornsby had heard all the stories about Old Pete, as he was called, but still wanted him for his team, an opinion shared by his coach Bill Killefer, the same Bill Killefer who had caught Alex for 11 years and knew that Alexander pitched better than anyone else sober or drunk. Five days after they picked up Alex, he pitched his first game, fittingly enough facing his old team, the Chicago Cubs. Giving up only four hits, he beat the Cubs in 10 innings, the first of the nine victories he was to contribute to the Cardinals pennant drive, a drive they capped off by out–hustling and out–pitching the Cincinnati Reds, winning the pennant by two games.

In that year's World Series against the fearsome Yankees, Alex took his regular turn in the second game and, pitching from memory, set down the last 21 Yankees after a third–inning single by Earle Combs, on his way to a 6–2 victory. Coming back in the sixth game, Alexander retired the first three men—a string of 24 in a row, second only to Don Larsen's 27 in a row in 1956—on his way to an eight–hit, 10–2 win, thus becoming the oldest pitcher to pitch a complete game in the World Series.

But, as a postscript, the best was yet to come. For in the seventh inning of the seventh game, with two outs, the bases loaded with Yankees, and Tony Lazzeri at bat, Rogers Hornsby replaced "Pop" Haines with Alexander, hollering "Alexander" somewhere in the direction of the bullpen. After a momentary delay, a familiar figure emerged from the left field bullpen, hat at a rakish angle and slouched over, as legend would have it, after celebrating all evening. Hornsby was to recall later, "Alexander could have been drunk for all I cared. Hell, I'd rather have him pitch a crucial game for me drunk than anyone I've ever known sober." All Alex said to Hornsby as the playing–manager handed him the ball was, "Well, I guess I'll have to take care of him then." And, ambling off in the direction of the mound, he threw four pitches to Lazzeri—one a long foul—before retiring him and clinching the Series for the team that had given an old, used–up 39–year–old pitcher the chance to show his stuff.

IN WHAT THREE WORLD SERIES DID THE TWO LEAGUE BATTING CHAMPIONS ONCE FACE EACH OTHER?

The World Series is at once the most prestigious and the most pretentious event on the American landscape. It is the most prestigious because no other event has captured the headlines nor the imagination of America so intensely for so long a period of time. It is pretentious because it holds itself out to be a competition of the best for the championship of the world, when it is, in reality, only for the championship of the northeastern quadrant of the Western Hemisphere. (However, baseball men, with more than a small measure of conceit, still proudly defend the Series as an international championship. Yankee owner George Steinbrenner provided the official party line to challenges of parochialism: "Well, we beat everybody who showed up.")

And sometimes the Series is worthy of all the hoopla and hype. As when the best show up to face each other, not only as teams but as individuals. And they have. Five times the home run leaders have faced each other in the World Series (1921, 1928, 1936, 1937, and 1956); two times the stolen base champions (1905 and 1938); eight times the Runs Batted In leaders (1909, 1923, 1924, 1926, 1927, 1928, 1929, and 1941); twice the leaders in doubles (1909 and 1975); four times the triples leaders (1925, 1927, 1928, and 1943); four times the pitching strikeout leaders (1905, 1930, 1931, and 1937); seven times the Earned Runs Average leaders (1905, 1906, 1915, 1927, 1943, 1945, and 1954); and three times the two batting champions were brought into head–to–head competition.

The three times the two batting champions faced each other were: in 1909, when Ty Cobb of the American League's Detroit Tigers and Honus Wagner of the National League's Pittsburgh Pirates led their teams into the Series; in 1931, when Al Simmons and Chick Hafey met, representing the Philadelphia A's and the St. Louis Cardinals; and in 1954, when Bobby Avila of the Indians and Willie Mays of the New York Giants met. In all three Series the National League won and all six batting champions batted less than their season average—ranging from Wagner hitting only .006 less than his 1909 leading average of .339 to Hafey hitting a full .182 points lower than his league–leading average of .349. In fact, since the Series started in 1903, only 26 batting leaders have appeared—14 in the National League and 12 in the American—and only four have out–hit their seasonal average in the Series.

WHO WAS THE LAST 300–GAME WINNER TO PITCH IN A WORLD SERIES?

Of those 18 bonafide and paid–up members of 300–wins club—Young, Johnson, Mathewson, Alexander, Spahn, Nichols, Galvin, Keefe, Clarkson, Plank, Carlton, Radbourn, Welch, Perry, Seaver, Grove, Wynn, and Niekro, in order of their number of wins—only 12 were still plying their trade after 1903, the dawn of the World Series. Or A. D., After the Dawn. Of those 12, neither Nichols or Niekro ever pitched in a Series. That leaves 10 modern–day pitchers who have won 300 games and played in a World Series. But of those 10 remaining pitchers with 300 wins, five pitched in the World Series *before* they won their 300th game, leaving only five 300–game winners ever to pitch in a Series: Cy Young, who, with 378 wins at that point in his career, pitched in the very first World Series, 1903; Christy Mathewson, who pitched in the 1912 Series with 312 lifetime wins, and in the 1913 Series with 337 wins; Walter Johnson, who pitched in the 1924 Series with 376 wins and in the 1925 Series with 396 wins, the most of any 300–game winner; Grover Cleveland Alexander, who pitched in the 1926 Series with 327 wins and in the 1928 Series with 364 wins; and, the last 300–game pitcher to appear in a World Series game, Steve Carlton, who pitched in the 1983 Series with exactly 300 wins to his credit.

6th Inning
The All-Star Game

WHO IS THE ONLY ALL–STAR MANAGER NOT TO USE ANY OF THE PLAYERS FROM HIS OWN TEAM?

There's an olde Southern colloquialism which holds, "You always dance with the person what brung you." And ever since Connie Mack and John McGraw managed the first All–Star teams back in 1933, with Mack starting the leading vote–getter Al Simmons in the outfield and pitching Lefty Grove from his own Philadelphia A's, and McGraw, the manager emeritus of the New York Giants, starting Bill Terry, his successor, at first and employing Lefty O'Doul as a pinch-hitter—that's exactly what's happened. With one exception. That came in 1943 when, in the first nighttime All–Star game in history, Yankee manager Joe McCarthy, managing his sixth All-Star team, bridled at the constant charge of "favoritism" hurled at him by the press. He took exception to the barb that he had used two Yankee catchers in the 1942 game—Bill Dickey and Buddy Rosar. Now there were strings in McCarthy's heart that did better not to be vibrated, and the charge of "favoritism" touched one of them. Deeply. And so Marse Joe determined not to use any of the six Yankees on the American League team—Bonham, Chandler, Dickey, Gordon, Keller, or Lindell—all the better to show his critics he could win without the Yankees. This was the only time no New York Yankee played in an All–Star Game. As they also say in the South, "It made no never mind," as the American League won, Yankees or no, 5–3.

WHAT FOUR MOST VALUABLE PLAYERS WERE NOT SELECTED FOR THE ALL–STAR GAME IN THE YEAR IN WHICH THEY WON THE AWARD?

The All-Star Game is an annual celebration of the game of baseball. Its rosters are chockful of the Marilyn Monroes of baseball, its superstars, showcasing their particular talents. And yet, occasionally, something happens that alters the well–laid plans of mice and baseball. One year, 1957, saw the rabid Cincinnati fans stuff the ballot boxes and elect a starting team of eight Cincinnati Reds for the National League's All-Star team. But Baseball Commissioner Ford Frick disallowed the bulk votes that came in at the last minute and restored three players who had been ahead before the final deluge of votes poured in: Stan Musial at first, Willie Mays in center field and Hank Aaron in right field in place of the "elected" trio of George Crowe, Gus Bell, and Wally Post.

But other times mere oversights could be blamed for the omission of a superstar. And the four times that has happened, the league's Most Valuable Player was left off the roster altogether. Hank Greenberg in 1935, Don Newcombe in 1956, Dave Parker in 1978, and Willie Stargell in 1979 were the superstars who somehow did not share in the midsummer celebration called the All-Star Game the year they won the Most Valuable Player award.

WHEN WAS THE ONLY TIME A TEAM HAD NO REPRESENTATIVE IN THE ALL-STAR GAME?

When the All-Star Game was first established in 1933, one of the governing rules was that each team be represented on its roster. And every year since, the roster has reflected this exclusivity, twice as exclusive as Noah, since only one member of each kind is guaranteed selection. However, there was one time when a team went unrepresented. That happened in 1972, when Texas Ranger shortstop Toby Harrah was selected to appear in place of the injured Luis Aparicio, was injured in turn and unable to appear. The American League went one more time to the well and came up with Bobby Grich of the Baltimore Orioles. But no provision was made to include a Texas Ranger, and so for the first, and only, time in All-Star Game history a team was left without representation.

WHO IS THE ONLY PLAYER TO HIT A HOME RUN IN AN ALL–STAR GAME AND NONE IN HIS REGULAR SEASON PLAY THAT SAME YEAR?

There have been 123 home runs in All-Star Game play through 1985, from Babe Ruth's blast in the inaugural 1933 Game through those hit by Brett, Carter, and Murphy in the 1984 Game. The 123 represent a sampling of those hit by some of the greatest hitters in the history of baseball, with the likes of Aaron, Banks, Bench, Colavito, DiMaggio, Foxx, Gehrig, Jackson, Killebrew, Kluszewski, Mantle, Mays, McCovey, Musial, Rice, Robinson, and Williams all hitting home runs, some during the year of their greatest home-run production. However, one player not only was not enjoying his greatest year in home-run production, he was experiencing a year in which he was to be shut out completely. Not counting pitchers, who as a group have never hit a home run in All–Star play and therefore are not countable, the one player who caught home-run lightning in a bottle was Dodger catcher Mickey Owen—he of "the dropped third strike" in the previous year's World Series—who hit a pinch-hit home run in the eighth of the 1942 Classic off American League pitcher Al Benton. That homer provided the National League with all its runs in a 3–1 loss to the American League and was Owen's only home run all year in 421 regular season at–bats and one All–Star game at–bat.

NAME THE ONLY PLAYER TO HAVE AT LEAST THREE HOME RUNS IN ALL–STAR, WORLD SERIES, AND LEAGUE CHAMPIONSHIP COMPETITION

"Baseball," said Bill Veeck, "is the only thing besides the paper clip that hasn't changed." But the paper clip now stands alone, especially after the 1969 season when baseball grafted on a League Championship Series at the end of the season to hold it together. And since that time, no less than 20 players have hit three home runs or more in League Championship competition. But only one, Johnny Bench, has hit at least three in All–Star, World Series, and League Championship play—with five in the Championship Series (one each in 1970, 1972, 1973, 1976, and 1979); five in the World Series (one each in 1970, 1972, 1975 and two in 1976); and three in All–Star Games (1969, 1971, and 1973).

WHAT PITCHER WON AN ALL–STAR GAME WITHOUT RETIRING ONE BATTER?

An olde Persian motto—which is redundant—reads: "Luck is infatuated with the efficient." None has ever been more efficient than Ken Ash of the Cincinnati Reds. He came on in relief on July 27, 1930 and threw just one pitch which resulted in a triple play, wiping three Cubs off the bases with one blow and giving him the win, his last in the majors. But All–Star pitcher Dean Stone comes close to Ash in the efficiency of results department, winning an All–Star Game on two pitches and without retiring one batter.

The scenario went something like this: the left–handed Stone, selected for All–Star service from the meager staff of the Washington Senators, was brought into the game by American

League manager Casey Stengel to relieve Chicago's right–handed pitcher Bob Keegan, facing Brooklyn's left–handed batter Duke Snider in the eighth inning of the 1954 Game. Stone found Red Schoendienst perched on third and Alvin Dark sitting on first, two out and the score 9–8 in favor of the National League. Snider took Stone's first two pitches, one wide for a ball and one for a strike. Then, as Stone went into his windup for his third pitch, Schoendienst, who had stood on third swaying like a reed in the soft summer breeze, took off for home, attempting to become the second man ever to steal home in an All–Star Game. (Pie Traynor in the 1934 Classic stole home on a double steal.) But Schoendienst miscalculated at a cost to himself and his team. Stone fired the ball to American League catcher Yogi Berra who applied the tag, a tag which stood up despite the protest of the two baseline coaches, Leo Durocher and Charlie Grimm, who argued that Stone had commited a balk. When the American League scored three runs in the bottom of the eighth, Stone, who had been replaced by Virgil Trucks, became the official winner, although he had only thrown two pitches and not officially retired one batter.

WHO WAS THE ONLY MAN TO BOTH PLAY IN AND UMPIRE AN ALL–STAR GAME?

Four men have returned to the scene of their playing triumphs in World Series games, reliving their sense of greatness as umpires in subsequent Classics—Bill Dineen, George Pipgras, Ed Rommell, and Lon Warneke. But only Warneke came back to umpire in an All–Star Game after playing in one—no, make that three. Warneke, a long–limbed right–hander who bore the label, "The Arkansas Humming Bird", in tribute to his origins, appeared in the inaugural All-Star game in 1933, relieving Carl

Hubbell in 1934 after his masterful five–straight strikeout performance and in 1936 came in to quell an American League uprising and save the National League's first All–Star Game win. Warneke, whose All–Star totals were somewhat less than those of the sterling standard, gave up 10 hits, six walks, and five runs in seven and one-third innings of work, with five strikeouts and one save. Then, representing the National League, Warneke came back to umpire the 1952 Game, the rain–shortened five–inning game in Philadelphia—the last National League player also to umpire in the Senior Circuit.

WHO ARE THE ONLY BROTHERS TO FACE EACH OTHER IN ALL–STAR COMPETITION?

Baseball makes estranged bedfellows, but never more so than when brothers play against each other. And despite the number of permutations available to baseball and its many brother acts, it has only happened once in All–Star competition. That came in the 1969 All–Star Game in Washington, D.C., when Carlos, representing the Chicago White Sox, and Lee, representing the Cincinnati Reds, both came to bat once and both went for the collar, making the May brothers the only brothers to both play and go 0–for–1 in the same All-Star Game.

NAME THE ONLY THREE PLAYERS TO MAKE THEIR LEAGUE'S ALL–STAR TEAM AFTER STARTING THE SEASON IN THE MINORS.

Ever since the All–Star Game jumped full–blown from the brow of Chicago sportswriter Arch Ward in 1933, the best players of each league have played against each other every year for baseball's version of bragging rights. There may have been some oversights in the voting; three members of the Hall of Fame whose active careers overlapped the All–Star Game never made their team's roster: Monte Irvin, Ted Lyons, and Paul Waner. But by and large, the All-Star Game has usually showcased the best available talent on major league rosters of each year. And sometimes the game showcased talent that wasn't even on the rosters at the beginning of the year. The three men who made it without benefit of starting the year on a major league roster are Don Schwall, who made the 1961 American League team even though he had started the year with Seattle, of the Pacific Coast League, Don Newcombe who made the 1949 National League team but started the year with Montreal, and Alvin Davis of Seattle, who made the 1984 National League team although he started the year playing for Salt Lake City. Bill Dawley almost qualified in 1983, but although he started spring training in Houston's minor league camp, he made it to Houston by Opening Day—and then to the All–Star Game.

WHO IS THE ONLY PLAYER TO REPRESENT FOUR DIFFERENT TEAMS ON ALL–STAR ROSTERS?

Oscar Wilde once wrote, "Three addresses always inspire confidence . . . even in tradesmen." And while no less than 17 men have been elected to All–Star teams with three different "addresses," "Goose" Gossage saw Oscar and raised him one by appearing on the All–Star roster in the uniforms of four different teams: the Chicago White Sox for the American League in 1975, the Pittsburgh Pirates for the National League in 1977, the New York Yankees for the American League in 1978 and 1980, and the San Diego Padres in 1984.

WHEN WAS THE ONLY TIME THE TWO STARTING PITCHERS IN THE ALL–STAR GAME WERE ALSO THE STARTING PITCHERS IN THE FIRST GAME OF THAT YEAR'S WORLD SERIES?

Since the first All-Star Game back in 19–aught–33, there have been almost as many starting pitchers as there have been games. But the odds that the best pitchers in both circuits would meet again in that year's World Series and start against each other in the first game of the fall classic are almost as long as they would be for the two opposing teams to field the exact same batting orders, position–for–position—a 362,880–to–1 possibility. However, it did happen. Once. In the 1939 All–Star Game, Red Ruffing of the American League, a 20–game winner his last three years and on his way to his fourth straight 20–game season, took the mound at Yankee Stadium, and Paul Derringer, the ace of the Cincinnati Reds' staff, on his way to a 25–game season, opposed him for the National League. Almost three months later, the two would once again face each other in the first game of the 1939 World Series as the Yankees met the Reds. Ironically, the first game of the 1939 Series also took place at Yankee Stadium, making Ruffing and Derringer the only two starting pitchers in the All–Star Game who also started the first game of that year's World Series *at the same ballpark.*

NAME THE ALL–STAR GAME IN WHICH THE WINNING AND LOSING PITCHERS WERE THE TALLEST PITCHERS, COMBINED, TO FIGURE IN A MAJOR LEAGUE DECISION.

Although pitcher Eppa Rixey is the tallest player in the Hall of Fame at 6′5″ and Johnny Gee, who pitched for the Pittsburgh Pirates and the New York Giants between 1939 and 1946, the tallest pitcher ever to take the mound in a major league game at 6′9″, the game in which the tallest winning and losing pitcher, combined, occurred in the 1955 All–Star Classic in Milwaukee.

In that 12–inning Game, Milwaukee's hometown hero, 6′8″ Gene Conley, came in to pitch to the American League in the top of the 12th and struck out Al Kaline, Mickey Vernon, and Al Rosen in succession. In the bottom of the 12th, the first pitch from Frank Sullivan, the 6′6½″ Boston Red Sox right–hander, to Stan Musial ended up in County Stadium's right–field bleachers, somewhere in the direction of Racine, making Sullivan the tallest losing and Conley the tallest winning pitcher, combined, in one game in major league history.

Ironically, five years later, after the 1960 season, the Boston Red Sox traded the same Frank Sullivan to the Philadelphia Phillies for the same Gene Conley, straight up—making the trade of these two men the tallest ever made.

NAME THE FIRST MAN IN ALL–STAR HISTORY TO HAVE A CAREER 1.000 BATTING AVERAGE IN MORE THAN ONE GAME.

All three DiMaggio brothers—Joe, Dom, and Vince—had two things in common; they all had the same middle name, Paul, and they all played in the All–Star Game. Joe, a seamless centerfielder for more than a decade-and-a-half, played in 11 games and hit .255. His little brother, Dom, who, at least in Boston, was rumored to have been better than Joe, played in six games and hit .353. But it was the oldest of the three, Vince, who made All–Star history. Vince, who had once played for Casey Stengel at Boston in 1938—where Casey was heard to remark, "Vince was the only player I saw who could strike out three times in one game and not be embarrassed. He'd walk into the clubhouse whistling. Everybody would be feeling sorry for him, but Vince thought he was doing good."—went on to play with Cincinnati and Pittsburgh where he finally came into his own, despite leading the National League in strikeouts three straight years. Still, he made All–Star teams in 1943 and 1944. Playing in both Games, Vince had three—count'em three—hits in three times at bat, a single, a triple and a home run, for an All–Star Average over the two Games of 1.000, the first man ever to do so. He was later matched by Willie Davis and Tim McCarver, both of whom also had three hits in three at-bats over two All-Star Games.

7th Inning
The 7th-Inning Stretch

IN WHAT TWO YEARS WERE THERE TWO TRIPLE CROWN WINNERS?

Baseball's Triple Crown is, like the proper making of a martini, the correct mating of ingredients at preciously the right moment. In a martini those ingredients, or "ingrediments" as Pogo would call them, are gin, vermouth, and occasionally, if someone doesn't mind the intrusion of other elements, an olive or two. In baseball those elements are the batting title, the home–run crown, and leadership in runs batted in. Throughout baseball history there have been but 14 triple crown winners—Ted Williams and Rogers Hornsby as the only repeaters—with Paul Hines winning the first one back in the dark ages of 1878 and Carl Yasztemski winning the last in 1967. And twice there have been two winners of the Triple Crown: the first time coming in 1933, when Jimmie Foxx won it in the American League and Chuck Klein won it in the National. The other time? To find that you must remember that baseball "borrowed" the phrase Triple Crown from horse racing when sportswriter Charlie Hatton of the *Morning Telegraph* linked the Kentucky Derby, the Preakness and the Belmont Stakes into one tag phrase. And so, since the term Triple Crown has been adopted from horse racing, it is only fair that horse racing become part of this hybred answer. In 1937 War Admiral won horse racing's Triple Crown and Joe Medwick won baseball's version of the same, the only other year in which there have been two Triple Crown winners.

WHO CAUGHT HANK AARON'S 715TH HOME RUN?

The trivia set, like any other set—whether it be the jet set or the TV set—tends to get trendy. A few years back the question that reigned as the most titillating and traveled amongst the trivia set was, "Who played for the Brooklyn Dodgers, the New York Rangers, and the New York Knicks in the same year?" The answer was Gladys Goodding, the organist. A year or so ago, Gladys's achievement had been replaced, at least in and around Detroit, with the question, "What Detroit native played with both the lions and the tigers?" The laughable answer was, "Clyde Beatty, the animal trainer." And this season's question has quickly become, "Who caught Hank Aaron's 715th home run?" But this time the question distinguishes itself from the others, inasmuch as the answer is a quasi-legitimate one, "Tom House, the Atlanta Braves' relief pitcher." He caught the ball while in the bullpen, thus joining Sal Durante, the fan who caught Roger Maris's 60th homer, as one of the two great catchers in the by and by.

WHO IS THE ONLY MAJOR LEAGUE BALL PLAYER TO BE BORN IN A TOWN WITH THE SAME NAME AS HIS OWN?

The variations on the theme are endless: Elmer Cleveland was born in Washington, D.C.; Herb Washington in Flint, Michigan; and Silver Flint in Philadelphia, Pennsylvania. Preston Gomez was born in Central Preston, Cuba. But none carried the same surname as the town of their origin. Only one major leaguer has. He is Estel Crabtree, who roamed the outfields on an intermittent basis for the Cincinnati Reds and St. Louis Cardinals between 1929 and 1944. Crabtree, born in Crabtree, Ohio, is the only major leaguer ever born in a town with the same name as his own. One other came close. Flint Rhem, the old pitcher for the St. Louis Cardinals, was born in Rhems, South Carolina, a town he claimed was named after his ancestors. However, Rhem was given to such flights of fancy that anything he said made some sense. Take the story of his supposed "kidnapping," for instance. Pitching for the Cardinals during the time when Prohibition lay heavy on the land, Rhem would more than occasionally slip through the fingers of its all enveloping hand. It was on one such occasion that Rhem disappeared from the team for days. Reappearing, he claimed that he had been "kidnapped" and that the kidnappers had locked him in a hotel room and forced him to drink great quantities of liquor at the point of a gun. Branch Rickey, the general manager of the Cardinals, could only shake his head at his favorite tosspot's story and mutter, "You couldn't disprove his story by the way he smelled."

WHAT MAJOR LEAGUE PLAYER HAD THE LONGEST COMPLETE NAME?

While it may have been Shakespeare who said, "What's in a name?" he might just as easily have said, "What's not in a name?" when it came to the full name of former San Francisco third baseman Al Gallagher whose full moniker was Alan Mitchell Edward George Patrick Henry Gallagher, a major league handle with 45 characters in all. He was called "Dirty Al" for short—but not for long, his career lasting only slightly longer than the recitation of his name, just 442 major league games in four years. Gallagher's name was a combination of all six boys' names his father had saved up for a son–to–be. But after waiting so long for his first–born, Gallagher *Père* decided to give his infant son a name that sounded like the reading of a train schedule rather than wait any longer.

Two other players come close in the longest name category: Bruno Betzel, an infielder with the St. Louis Cardinals from 1914 through 1918, who was originally christened Christian Frederick Albert John Henry Davis Betzel, a total of 44 letters; and the pitcher Calvin Coolidge Julius Caesar Tuskahoma McLish, a mouthful that takes care of but 41 letters, the same number as Alejandro Alexander Aparicio Elroy Carrasquel. Not even close was Saturnino Orestes Arrieta Armas Minoso, who finished with a mere 34 characters and an honorable mention in the longest name sweepstakes.

But even Alan Mitchell Edward George Patrick Henry Gallagher cannot hold a candle to the longest name in movie history, 67 letters in all: Rudolpho Pierre Filibert Alphonzo Rafae Gugliemi di Valentina d'Antonguolla, better known by his *nom de screen*, Rudolph Valentino.

WHAT AMERICAN LEAGUE RECORD WAS SET—AND MAJOR LEAGUE RECORD TIED—ON THE VERY FIRST DAY OF AMERICAN LEAGUE PLAY, NEVER TO BE BROKEN?

Those tireless old gentlemen who used to recount the beginnings of baseball, as we now know it, were oft wont to invoke the name of Byron Bancroft Johnson, better known as just plain "Ban," the founding father of the American League. Johnson, as some of the more lucid might recall, had started as a sportswriter at the old–old Cincinnati *Commercial Gazette.* But like all kids who grew up in the 1860s when the world of baseball revolved around the Cincinnatti Red Stockings—and vice versa—he not only mainlined baseball but yearned for the opportunity to play a bigger role in it. It was while Johnson was covering the Cincinnati Reds of the early 1890s that he struck up a friendship with its manager and first baseman Charlie Comiskey, and that opportunity knocked. For Comiskey was then in the twilight of his long career and looking for greener diamonds and pastures to conquer: Johnson had both. Over drinks at Cincinnati's Ten Minute Club—so called because members made a regular practice of calling a waiter at the expiration of each 10–minute interval—the two hatched a plan to revive the old Western League, a league which was to be expanded in 1900 into the American League.

Johnson determined to go "Major League" in 1901, advertising his new league with what sounded like a campaign slogan: "Clean baseball, beer, and plenty of 25¢ seats." Somehow his campaign oratory swayed the emotions of several, not unimportantly the eight men who put up the money for the fledgling franchises in the eight American League cities—Baltimore, Boston, Chicago, Cleveland, Detroit, Milwaukee, Philadelphia, and Washington. Concurrent with his sloganeering, Johnson went electioneering, trying to win over some of those ballplayers from the "other" league, the National League, who might provide some credibility to the group of has–beens, never–wases and names that weren't even household names in their own households who were then peopling the rosters of his eight teams. He was immediately successful, luring away a superstar–to–be Napoleon Lajoie on a smile, a shoeshine and the promise of $50 more a season. Now he was ready to start, and start he did, in grand fashion, rolling out his opening day festivities like a circus caravan over a two–day period, Wednesday April 24, in two cities and Thursday, April 25, in two more.

The first American League game ever to be played in Detroit came on the back–end of the roll–out, a game which drew an estimated 9,000 curious fans to old Bennett Park to watch their new team, the Tigers. Johnson couldn't have choreographed it better. For with Milwaukee winning 13–4 in the bottom of the ninth, Detroit erupted for 10 runs and victory, 14–13. During the uprising, one batter, first baseman Frank "Pop" Dillon, hit two doubles, giving him a total of four for the afternoon. It was to be the first time in American League history, naturally enough, that a player had hit four doubles in one afternoon.

And both records—two doubles in one inning and four doubles in an afternoon—were records that have stood the test of time, equaled but never surpassed in the following 85 years of American League play. And although Johnson, even now in that great commissioner's office in the sky, would never admit to the existence of that "other" league, he has never been surpassed by them either!

NAME THE SIX MAJOR LEAGUE BALLPLAYERS WHOSE LAST NAMES ARE SPELLED THE SAME BACKWARD AS WELL AS FORWARD.

A palindrome is defined as "a word, verse or sentence that is the same when read backward or forward," as in the time–honored one attributed to Napoleon upon his first seeing his place of exile: "Able was I ere I saw Elba." This same masturbatory exercise works as well with ballplayers as it does with Napoleon, or to paraphrase Gene Mauch, "What did he hit anyway?"

The six major league players who are able to spell their surnames the same way backward as they do forward are: Dick Nen of the Los Angeles Dodgers, Washington Senators, and Chicago Cubs (1963–1970); Toby Harrah of the Washington Senators, Texas Rangers, and New York Yankees (1969–1984); Truck Hannah of the New York Yankees (1918–1920); Eddie Kazak of the St. Louis Cardinals and Cincinnati Reds (1948–1952); Johnny Reder of the Boston Red Sox (1932); and the newest member of this exclusive club, Mark Salas of the St. Louis Cardinals (1985).

Added to these name palindromes are the interchangeable name, like Gorman Thomas and Thomas Gorman, and the playing palindrome. The most notable playing palindrome are those of Sammy Ellis's 1965 pitching record which shows 22 wins, 222 hits allowed and two saves and two shutouts and Greg Goossen's six–year lifetime batting totals which show 111 base hits, 33 runs, 44 RBI's and 11 pinch hits for a lifetime .383 slugging average. Spelled backwards that reads 22 wins, 22 hits, etc. . . .

WHAT TWO FORDHAM SECOND BASEMEN BOTH WENT ON TO BECOME CARDINALS?

Just as the current bar favorite, "What four American presidents are not buried in the United States?" presupposes they're all dead—and they're not (the answer being Nixon, Ford, Carter, and Reagan)—this question presupposes that both Fordham second basemen became St. Louis Cardinals. They didn't.

Second baseman Frankie Frisch graduated directly from the Fordham campus in 1919 to star with the New York Giants. The man known, appropriately enough, as "The Fordham Flash," broke in as a pinch hitter for Hal Chase and later became the playing manager for the St. Louis Cardinals' famed "Gashouse Gang." Ten years earlier Frankie Spellman, later to become Francis Cardinal Spellman of the New York Archdiocese, was the second–string Fordham second baseman behind Jack Coffey, who played for the Braves and Red Sox and became Fordham's athletic director, making Frisch and Spellman the two Fordham second basemen to go on to become Cardinals. Of sorts.

WHAT WAS THE NAME OF THE RIGHT FIELDER IN THE ABBOTT AND COSTELLO "WHO'S ON FIRST" SKIT?

First introduced in the 1945 Universal movie *The Naughty Nineties*, the "Who's on First?" vaudeville skit became as much a part of baseball as it became a part of Abbott and Costello. In the skit, Bud Abbott as Dexter Broadhurst, manager of the Wolves, tries to answer the questions of the inquisitive peanut butcher Sebastian Dinwiddle, played by Lou Costello, "Who's on first?"

To Dinwiddle–Costello's constant query, "Who's on first?," Broadhurst–Abbott answers with a variety of answers–cum–player designations, trying mightily to impress upon Costello that "*Who's* on first" and "*What's* on second." But Costello cannot fathom the team's alignment and finally, in frustration, cries out, "I don't care," to which he is informed that he has just identified the shortstop. The members of this confusing but memorable team are: First base, Who; Second base, What; Third base, I Don't Know; Shortstop, I Don't Care; Pitcher, Tomorrow; Catcher, Today; Left field, Why; and Center field, Because. But, like the pitcher in Casey at the Bat, who also is never mentioned, there is no right fielder. And so the above question is not, "*What* was the name of the Rightfielder? inasmuch as

What was the second baseman. Nor can the answer be, "I don't know," since that is the name of the third baseman. The answer, simply stated, is that there is no Right fielder mentioned. Why? I don't know! And I don't care!

WHAT TWO ROOMMATES HAD THE SHORTEST COMBINED LAST NAMES IN BASEBALL HISTORY?

There have been several players with only three letters in their last names—Mel Ott, Emil Yde, and Joey Jay come to mind. But Billy Cox and Preacher Roe were two whose three–letter last names were combined not only as teammates but as roommates during several years of their seven–year stay with the Brooklyn Dodgers. This stay began for both in 1948 when they were involved in the same trade from Pittsburgh and ended for both in 1954 when they were both again involved in the same trade to Baltimore, making them the two players in the same trade to have the shortest combined last names. Twice.

WHO WERE THE ONLY TWO MAJOR LEAGUE BALLPLAYERS BORN ON FEBRUARY 29TH?

Leap years are those years which can be divided evenly by four, except years that mark the even hundred, such as 1900. The only century years qualifying are those years which can be divided by 400, such as the year 2000. The extra 366th day, added to the calendar to make the calendar year nearly the same as the solar year, is added at the end of February, giving us February 29th once every four years. It was on such an extra calendar day in 1904 that John Leonard Roosevelt "Pepper" Martin was born in Temple, Okla., and on yet another February 29th in the leap year of 1924 that Albert Leonard "Flip" Rosen first saw the light of day. Ironically, both would close out their major league careers during another leap year: Martin in 1944 and Rosen in 1956. Other noteworthy birthdays include those of Dave Winfield, born on October 3, 1951, the same day Bobby Thomson hit his "Shot Heard 'Round the World" in the 1951 play–offs, and Mike Jorgensen, born August 16, 1948, the same day Babe Ruth died; and Jeff Lahti, born October 3, 1956, the day of Larsen's perfect game. Two players have even died on February 29th: Rebel Oakes (1948) and Lena Blackburne (1968).

WHAT PLAYER HAD HIS COMPLETE BIRTHDAY ON THE BACK OF HIS UNIFORM?

Bill Veeck is most often remembered as the man who brought a midget to the plate—a fact Veeck himself acknowledged, quipping that his tombstone would undoubtedly bear the inscription, "He did most for the little people." But it was also Veeck who introduced one of the greatest aids for viewer involvement, not to mention aids for incremental program sales, when he first put the names of his Chicago White Sox players on the backs of their uniforms, even going so far as to purposely alter the spelling of Ted Kluszewski's name—all in the name of added publicity, of course.

One member of the ChiSox whose name appeared on his jersey was Carlos May, who joined the team in 1968, after Veeck had departed for the first time. May, one of only eight players whose names are incidentally, also that of a month of the year, (all eight being May), wore number 17 under his name, thus billboarding his complete birthday, May 17. One other player billboarded not his birthday, but his hometown on the back of his uniform. Bill Voiselle, who pitched for the New York Giants, Boston Braves, and Chicago Cubs from 1942 through 1950, was the pride and joy of Ninety–Six, S.C. (population 1,345 in Greenwood County). So it was only right and proper that he be assigned a uniform with the number "96" on the back of it, advertising the town's existence better than any flyer the Chamber of Commerce could ever have developed.

NAME THE ONLY PLAYER EVER TO HAVE A TOWN NAMED AFTER HIM.

Pete Rose may have had a street named after him, Babe Ruth a plaza, and even Dizzy Dean a mosquito (The Mastophora Dizzydeani, which throws a straight globule of spit out at its prey and then reels it in), but only Jim Thorpe ever had a town named after him. What's that, you say, Jim Thorpe a baseball player? Depending upon what yellowing news clips one reads, one can find references attesting to Thorpe's excellence on the gridiron as a two–time All–American at Carlisle back in 1911, and 1912, or as the first superstar of the embryonic National Football League or as the Decathlon Gold Medalist in the 1912 Olympics. But one can find precious few describing his association with baseball. And probably with good reason, for Thorpe inhabited the outfields of the New York Giants, the Cincinnati Reds, and the Boston Braves for six relatively undistinguished years, a promise unkept, in spite of the greatness hinted at and his awesome talent. But for one magic moment on the afternoon of May 2, 1917, Thorpe managed to come to the baseball trivia stage front and center by getting the infield single that broke up baseball's greatest pitching duel, the 10–inning double no–hit game between Chicago's "Hippo" Vaughn and Cincinnati's Fred Toney.

And so it was in 1954, when the town of Mauch Chunk, Pa. decided, in hopes of adding a bloom to its faded rose, to rename itself "Jim Thorpe," Pa. that the first and only town ever named for a professional ballplayer came into being. Unfortunately, as a postscript, although Thorpe's body was transferred to Jim Thorpe, Pa. and buried alongside Route 903, the promised fame and tourism never materialized, another promise unkept in the saga of the man once called by the King of Sweden, "The greatest athlete in the world."

WHAT WAS THE ONLY LAST NAME IN BASEBALL HISTORY TO CONTAIN ALL FIVE VOWELS.

Vowels are damnably important, not only to the English language, but also to its writers, such as mystery writer Rex Stout who consciously distributed the vowels in the name of his detective, Nero Wolfe, to the pattern of those in the name of his hero Sherlock Holmes, making sure that the "o" followed the "e" in the first name and versa–vice in the last name, the "e" following the "o." The five vowels, *A, E, I, O,* and *U* come together ever so infrequently, all appearing in some words like "facetious," and all in the right order, too, then declining to the point where some words don't even contain one such as in the word "rhythm." Sports players' names are a little different. Years ago Temple University once had a basketball player named Bill Mikvy, appropriately called, "The Owl with No Vowel." And, baseball has had two players with all five vowels in their last name. Discounting that small band of men whose first name was

Aurielo, which contained all five vowels, and former Minnesota catcher Hank Isquierdo, who had all the vowels in his first name combined with his surname, the only two players with all five vowels in their last name are Ed Figueroa, who pitched for the New York Yankees and Oakland A's from 1974 through 1981, and his namesake but no relation Jesus Figueroa, who played for the Chicago Cubs in 1980.

WITH THE NOTABLE EXCEPTION OF EDDIE GAEDEL, WHO WAS THE LIGHTEST MAN EVER TO PLAY IN THE MAJORS?

Bill Veeck had promised "something special" on that bright, clear August Sunday in 1951 to bring out the loyal St. Louis Browns fans who had continued to show their appreciation for the Browns' play on the field by failing to show up in record numbers. That "something special" turned out to be a 65–pound, 3′7″ midget named Eddie Gaedel, who pinch hit for the Browns' outfielder, Frank Saucier, and walked on four straight pitches from the pitcher, Bob Cain of the Detroit Tigers, who was convulsed at the sight of his size. Gaedel thus staked his claim to any Hall of Fame that wanted him: the Trivia Hall of Fame, Ripley's *Believe It or Not* Hall of Fame or even the Lightweight Hall of Fame.

But until Gaedel took his miniplace in the batter's box that day, the honor for the lightest ballplayer in the history of baseball had belonged to Johnny Evers, who had been but 95 pounds when he first broke in with the Chicago Cubs in 1902, there to partake in the first Tinker–to–Evers–to–Chance double play, September 15, 1902. Later to become part of the famous Tinker–to–Evers–to Chance infield combination, the diminutive 5′9″ Evers looked more like a baseball bat with a thyroid condition than a ballplayer, although differing radically in design. But even then there was something about this walking case of malnutrition that hinted at greatness; his combativeness and leadership helped the Cubs to realize his potential. That potential would continue for the next 17 years as Evers' stature was increasingly made all the greater by the ever–lengthening shadow of his achievements, achievements that would ultimately carry him to the Hall of Fame where he became the lightest member enshrined. The overall impression left of Evers was that it was not the size of the ballplayer in the game but the size of the game in the ballplayer, a characteristic that would lead poet Ogden Nash to write, "E is for Evers/His Jaw in advance/Never Afraid/To Tinker with Chance."

WHO IS THE ONLY WOMAN TO COME TO BAT IN A MAJOR LEAGUE GAME?

Folklore is filled with the exploits of women who did something or other on the diamond: Mrs. George (Eleanor) Engle, who worked out with Harrisburg of the Inter–State in 1952 and sat in the dugout during the Harrisburg–Lancaster game of June 22, 1952, but who was never signed to a contract after feminine performers were officially barred from playing in organized baseball; Virne Beatrice "Jackie" Mitchell, pitcher, Chattanooga of the Southern Association, who, on April 2, 1931, saw service as a relief pitcher in the first inning of an exhibition game and struck out both Babe Ruth and Lou Gehrig before walking Tony Lazzeri; and, of course, Babe Didrickson, who pitched exhibition ball during the early 1930s, often against major league players.

But the only woman who actually came to the plate in a major league baseball game was Kitty Burke. In one of the first night games in baseball history, Wednesday, July 31, 1935, an uncontrollable sellout crowd used a people–horn to pack into Cincinnati's Crosley Field to see the Reds host the St. Louis Cardinals. The overflow crowd stood 10–deep around the diamond and occupied the right and left field corners, causing no end to the confusion as players had to battle their way not only to the ball but to the dugout as well. During the seventh inning, Kitty Burke grabbed the bat out of the hands of the Reds' Babe Herman and made her way up to the batter's box, bat in hand. Paul Dean, who was standing on the mound awaiting the entry of Herman, was more than somewhat confused by the entry of the new player. Nevertheless, he accomodated her by throwing her a pitch, and for the next year Miss Burke would tour the burlesque circuit billed as, "The Only Woman To Bat in the Major Leagues."

NAME THE BALL PARK IN WHICH THE MOST HOMERS WERE HIT DURING A SEASON.

When John Grabowski posed this question in his *Baseball Trivia Newsletter,* most of the respondents proffered the answer "Wrigley Field." They received partial credit. The answer *is* Wrigley Field, but not *that* Wrigley Field. It's the one 2,200 miles West. For back in 1961, when the American League expanded for the first time, they brought in two teams, the new—not to be confused with the old, who were confused enough as it was—Washington Senators and the Los Angeles Angels. In an agreement with the grand poohbah of West Coast baseball, not to mention baseball in general, Walter O'Malley, the new owner of the Angels, Gene Autry, agreed to play the Angels' 1961 games at Wrigley Field, the 20,500–seat home of the former Pacific Coast League club and then move into Chavez Ravine in 1962. But what a year 1961 was! The expansion Angels hit 122 home runs and their visitors, accepting their hospitality, added 126 more of their own for a major league record of 248 home runs in one park in one season. Leon "Daddy Wags" Wagner had 19 round–trippers to lead the Angels, while Baltimore Orioles first baseman, Jim Gentile, had the most by a visitor, eight. And despite nine games in the overly friendly confines of Wrigley Field, Roger Maris only had two of his record-setting 61 in the little bandbox.

WHO ARE THE ONLY THREE MEN TO PLAY IN BOTH THE MAJORS AND IN THE NATIONAL FOOTBALL LEAGUE FOR TWO CONSECUTIVE YEARS?

While it might offend our residual memory, there was once a time when the baseball and football seasons had a distinct line of demarcation, not overlapping to the point of indistinction where the boundaries are so blurred that it is almost impossible to determine where one season ends and the other begins. And, in those days of yore, it was possible for an all–around athlete to participate in both. From the day when 11 representatives of fledgling football clubs met in a Hupmobile agency in Canton, Ohio, to form what is now the National Football League—even though, according to one of those in attendance, George Halas, "A fee of $100 was charged for membership and there wasn't $100 in the room . . ."—there have been 43 men who have played in both the majors and the National Football League.

One of those 43 was Halas, himself, who had started the 1919 season as the right fielder for the New York Yankees, the year before Babe Ruth came over from the Red Sox to take up permanent possession. Another was Halas's starting quarterback, Charlie Dressen. And still a third was the first president of the NFL, Jim Thorpe. But none of those three—or others such as Charlie Berry, Garland Buckeye, Evar Swanson, and Hinkey

Haines, all of whom played in both the majors and the NFL—ever played two successive years in *both* professional leagues.

One of those who *did* was the only triple major–league level participant in baseball, football, and basketball. He was Ernie Nevers. Nevers, one of football's all–time greats, broke in the year following his unanimous selection as an All–American at Stanford, where he had been hailed as a "One-Man" Gang. Appearing as a pitcher in just 44 games for the St. Louis Browns in 1926, 1927, and 1928, Nevers posted a record of 6–12; his greatest achievement being a negative—giving up Babe Ruth's eighth and 41st home runs in his recordbreaking year of 1927. Fortunately, Nevers was far more successful in the NFL, where, playing for the Duluth Eskimos in 1926 (and 1927 and 1928 as well), he set the all–time professional scoring record, 40 points in one game.

The other two members of this exclusive triumverate, playing both major league baseball and NFL football for two successive years, are: Everett "Pid" Purdy, who played baseball for the 1926 Chicago White Sox and the 1927 Cincinnati Reds while moonlighting as a blocking back for the Green Bay Packers both years and Clarence "Ace" Parker, who played shortstop for the Philadelphia A's in 1937 and 1938 and as a running back for the Brooklyn (football) Dodgers in both years. Ironically, each of the three had more football points than base hits in major league play during those two years: Nevers having 12 hits and 102 points in 1926 and 1927, Purdy, having 28 hits and 30 points in the same two years, and Parker having 37 hits and 42 points in 1937 and 1938. Undoubtedly, they proved which side of the bread their sport was buttered on.

WHO HOLDS THE UNOFFICIAL RECORD FOR PASSING THE MOST RUNNERS ON THE BASE PATHS AND NEGATING THE MOST HOME RUNS IN ONE YEAR?

Ebbets Field was always a wondrous place to behold, a drafty old ball park, bordered by Montgomery Street, Sullivan Place, McKeever Place, and Bedford Avenue. However, its real location was in the hearts of loyal Brooklyn rooters who packed it every afternoon, 31,902 strong, in an early version of group therapy. There they hooted, whistled, stamped, and just cheered for their Dodgers heroes, so much so that sportswriter Dan Parker captured their rapture with the verse: "Summer or winter or any season, Flatbush fanatics don't need no reason. Leave us root for the Dodgers, Rodgers. That's the team for me." And before the Dodgers even became the beloved Bums, courtesy of a Willard Mullin cartoon, they were dubbed The Daffiness Boys for good and sufficient reasons.

Back then in the mid–1920s, a decade known as that "Era of Wonderful Nonsense," the Dodgers had a roster full of players who could best be described as life's losing stuntmen. But the most curious piece of goods of all, was a tall, angular outfielder who looked like a lost altar boy in search of a service, Floyd Caves "Babe" Herman. Herman was a strong, powerful hitter who could fetch home three runs with his bat and give up four with his glove and base running. His talents for base running were so legendary that Dazzy Vance gave him a nickname, "The Headless Horseman of Ebbets Field."

It was the most classic understatement since a Crow scout told Colonel Custer there might be trouble along the Little Big Horn. For although Herman could hit the ball a country mile—and, in fact, still holds the Dodger record for slugging percentage with a .557 average and the highest batting average ever by a Dodger with .393—he could undo all of that with his base running. On one occasion, August 15, 1926, Herman came to bat with Vance on second and Chick Fewster on first and clouted a ball somewhere in the direction of Montague Street. By the time the ball was retrieved and the dust had settled, there stood all three base runners on third, sort of an old–time Shriner's convention, with handshakes and headshakes all around. Another time, Gabby Street, then the manager of the St. Louis Cardinals and fast approaching his 49th birthday, inserted himself into the lineup as the starting catcher after 19 years of inactivity. Even after a 19–year hiatus, he was still able to throw out the only base runner who tried to steal on him—you guessed it!—Babe Herman. Whether Herman was trying to communicate with the fans or commune with nature, his head always seemed to be somewhere else. And so it was that twice in 1930—the first time on May 30 when Del Bissonette hit a home run, the second time on September 15 when Glenn Wright performed the same act—Herman, the unartful Dodger, was standing somewhere around the base paths. And both times, more intent on following the flight of the ball than the flow of the play, he was passed on the base paths by the two base runners trying mightily to make their way home to a rousing greeting at the plate—an unofficial record for being passed twice on the base paths in a single season.

There have been other times in baseball history when runners have lapped each other, negating homers. Perhaps the most famous time occurred on the night of May 26, 1959, when Hank Aaron, seeing that Felix Mantilla had scored on Joe Adcock's towering home run into the stand to break up Harvey Haddix's Perfect Game in the bottom of the 13th, left the base paths, negating Adcock's homer. Another time came on April 27, 1931 when Lyn Lary, seeing Washington Senator outfielder Sam Rice make a grandstand catch of Lou Gehrig's home run which had richocheted back out of the stands, misunderstood Joe McCarthy's furious arm–waving. He thought it just meant for him to slow down and take his position in the field on what he thought to be the third out, went to the dugout to get his glove, and thereby cost Gehrig a homer and the undisputed home run championship for the year. Not incidentally, it was also the last time Joe McCarthy ever coached from the third base coach's box. Specs Toporcer deprived himself of his first major league home run, one hit over the short right field fence at Philadelphia's Baker Bowl on June 12, 1922, when he passed teammate Doc Lavan between first and second. But none of them ever did it twice in a season, let alone a career.

WHO SHOT EDDIE WAITKUS?

In the movie *The Natural,* the protagonist, Roy Hobbs, bearing a startling resemblance to Robert Redford, is shot with a silver bullet by a mysterious woman in black he met on a train en route to Chicago. The scene is not original. The city of Chicago has witnessed two shootings of ballplayers—not to mention those hundreds in Cubs and White Sox uniforms who appear to be half–shot.

Back in 1932, Billy Jurges, then the second–year shortstop for the pennant–bound Cubs, was shot and wounded at Chicago's Carlos Hotel on July 6, 1932 by a show girl, Violet Popovich Valli. The matter was hushed up, euphemistically reported in newspapers as an "untimely injury". But whatever it was, the Cubs desperately needed a shortstop for their stretch drive. Thus it was that casting around for a replacement, the Cubs came up with Mark Koenig, then on the San Francisco Missions, where he had been relegated, like last season's suit, by the Detroit Tigers at the beginning of the year. Brought up on August 5, 1932, all Koenig did was anchor the infield, hit a solid .353 in 33 games, and provide the spark for the Yankee-Cub ugly feud that erupted into a full–fledged name–calling contest in the World Series that year when the Cubs only gave him a partial split of their pennant spoils. The crowning blow, in more ways than one, was Babe Ruth's so–called "shot" off Cub pitcher Charlie Root, when Ruth matched Root's thunder with his own lightning.

Seventeen years later, in another scene from *The Natural,* Philadelphia Phillies first baseman Eddie Waitkus received a note in his room at the Edgewater Beach Hotel in, you guessed it, Chicago, on the night of June 15, 1949, from a young woman he did not know, insisting that she see him in her room "as soon as possible" because of "something extremely important." Responding to the urgency of the note, Waitkus went to the room of one Ruth Ann Steinhagen who rewarded his presence with a shot to the chest from a secondhand rifle, a case of the fiction of *The Natural* following real life. Waitkus did recover. He was nursed back to health by a registered nurse who would ultimately become his wife, returning to the Phillies lineup in 1950 to help the Whiz Kids win the National League pennant. Ironically, both Waitkus in the 1950 World Series and Jurges in the 1932 Series would play on teams that lost in four games to the New York Yankees and both, in the World Series the year after they were shot, would get four hits, including one double. But, unlike Roy Hobbs, neither would get a home run.

WHO IS THE ONLY MAJOR LEAGUER TO PLAY IN A SUPER BOWL?

Baseball can count amongst its number one Heisman Trophy winner—Vic Janowicz, the Ohio State halfback who won the Heisman in 1950 and played 83 games for the Pittsburgh Pirates in 1953 and 1954—and three men who have appeared in a World Series game and in the Rose Bowl—Jackie Jensen, who played for the 1949 California Golden Bears and for the Yankees in the 1950 World Series; Chuck Essgian, who played for the 1952 Stanford team and in the 1959 Series for the Dodgers; and Earl "Greasy" Neale, who coached Washington and Jefferson College in the 1922 Rose Bowl game and played in the 1919 Series for Cincinnati. However, the only major league player to play in a Super Bowl was Tommy Brown, who had come directly to the Washington Senators in 1963 from the University of Maryland where he had starred in both football and baseball. But, after one anemic year with the Senators—a year in which he batted .147 with but five extra bases hits scattered among his 17 total hits—Brown, as jubilant as a martyr saved at the stake, jumped to the Green Bay Packers. There, as a member of their defensive backfield, he played on two winning Super Bowl teams in Super Bowls I and II, making him the only major leaguer ever to have played in the NFL Championship Game.

WHO IS THE ONLY MAJOR LEAGUER TO TACKLE O.J. SIMPSON AND HIT A HOME RUN OFF J. R. RICHARD?

One of yesteryear's favorite questions went something like this: "Name the only man to catch a touchdown pass from Y. A. Tittle and hit a home run off Sandy Koufax." And for years the answer was rendered up thusly: "Alvin Dark." However, one writer, Joe Healey in *Inside Sports* magazine, put the lie to the question by pointing out, "The popular answer is Alvin Dark. Again, the popular answer is wrong. The correct answer is nobody. While Dark was a superb athlete, he would have had to have been Superman to pull off that feat. For Dark to have caught a pass from Tittle, it would have had to have been a long one because they weren't at Louisiana State University at the same time. Dark played in the LSU backfield in 1942, Tittle from 1944-1947." Even Dark himself, when asked the question by *The New York Times* sportswriter Leonard Koppett, anguished, "I'm so tired of denying it, that now I just accept it."

And so, as one of those who pleads *mea culpa* for past misdeeds in disseminating "wrong" trivia in his previous book, *Who Was Harry Steinfeldt? And Other Baseball Trivia Questions,* this writer humbly proffers a substitute one: "Who is the only major leaguer to tackle O. J. Simpson and hit a home run off J. R. Richard?" The answer is Steve Garvey, who as a football star at Michigan State played against Simpson's Southern Cal team and, as a superstar first baseman in the National League, faced J. R. Richard. Mr. Healey, your turn!

NAME THE ONLY MAJOR LEAGUE PLAYER IN HISTORY WHO HAD TO TAKE A TETANUS SHOT AFTER AN ON–THE–FIELD BRAWL.

There have been brawls and then there have been brawls. Some have been beauts, like the time when Juan Marichal took a disliking to John Roseboro and a bat to his head, in that order. He produced a ringing in Roseboro's ears that rivaled those heard by bellhops. Or the time when Ruben Gomez thought the lion named Joe Adcock was sleeping because he didn't hear him roar and plunked him in the ribs with the ball, causing a bat–brandishing Adcock to chase Gomez across the infield and into the dugout, running as if he were trying to get out of the way of an onrushing storm. Which he was. Or even those push–comes–to–shove matches between Billy Martin and Clint Courtney or Billy Martin and Jim Brewer or Billy Martin and Jimmy Piersall or Billy Martin and just about anyone short of Hulk Hogan imaginable. But the only time a player ever had to take a tetanus shot came during a donneybrook in Pittsburgh between the Cincinnati Reds and the Pirates on July 14, 1974, one brought on by an exchange of pleasantries and beanballs.

The whole affair had started with Reds' pitcher Jack Billingham swatting his opposite number, Pirates' pitcher Bruce Kison, with a fastball that one heard with an audible thud. Both dugouts emptied as the players traded insults and in–your–face threats. Then, just as everything was quieting down, aided and abetted by the peacemaking efforts of the two managers, Sparky Anderson of the Reds and Danny Murtaugh of the Pirates, an inadvertent spark set off an eruption. Or, more accurately stated, an inadvertent Sparky. For Anderson, then more concerned with the players' whereabouts than the whereabouts of a foot or two, unintentionally stepped on one belonging to Ed Kirkpatrick, the Pirate first baseman. Kirkpatrick retaliated by pushing Anderson back. Reds' Andy Kosco, then ending his career as a spear carrier, decided that Kirkpatrick wanted it in the worst way, and delivered it accordingly, punching Kirkpatrick in the mouth. The fight was on in earnest. And in the middle of it was that one-man volcano, the Reds' relief man, Pedro Borbon, who had gained some notoriety in the previous year's National League Championship Series by insinuating himself into the punching match between Pete Rose and Bud Harrelson. Picking up a hat he thought was his own, Borbon found out, instead, it belonged to the Mets Buzz Capri, and took a bite out of the brim. Now, Borbon unconditionally surrendered to his emotions and began his routine again, this time grabbing Pirates' pitcher Daryl Patterson and throwing him to the ground, there to perform his own tribal rites. Knowing Patterson to be a sucker for a rite, Borbon proceeded to pull out Patterson's hair by the clump and bite him, tearing a chunk of flesh out of the poor Pirate pitcher's side. When order was restored, there was much to be attended to: players to be ejected, fines to be levied, and one tetanus shot to be given to Daryl Patterson, courtesy of Pedro Borbon, baseball's Count Dracula.

WHAT BAT SET TWO NATIONAL LEAGUE RECORDS—11 YEARS APART?

In the long history of baseball, the bat has come to be the most important instrument in the game, even taking on a life of its own. To some it serves as a blasting cap, to others a mechanical implement with its own instincts, and to still others a device with all the consistency of wet blotting paper—or, as clichésmiths would have it, "A bat with a hole in it." Ever since that day when Pete Browning had Hillerich & Bradsby fashion a bat for him, forever lending his name to the Louisville Slugger, down through Babe Ruth's favorite bat, The Black Betsy, and up to the present, the bat has had a personal history. In the hands of Hack Miller of the old Chicago Cubs, reputedly the strongest man ever to play baseball, it was a 42–inch weapon, the heaviest ever; in the case of Joe Adcock, it was a borrowed bat, one so heavy he could barely lift it, which enabled him to hit four home runs and a double in one game in 1954; and for Bill Terry, it meant just two bats during the 1930 season in which he hit .401.

Then there was the bat of Tom Hendryx, former American League outfielder, which during his less–than–illustrious career, had barely been used. It had been lying fallow since 1921, until both Pie Traynor—who had a propensity for discarded bats—and Paul Waner employed it in 1927. That bat allowed Waner to lead the National League with a .380 average and Traynor to hit .342 as they led the Pirates to the National League pennant. It could even be the bats that Joe Tinker borrowed from his teammates, sawing off the handles so that he could grip them and then trying mightily to return the damaged merchandise to the unappreciative lenders.

But the bat that set National League history 11 years apart was the most illustrious bat in baseball—even including the Lightning bat toted by Roy Hobbs in *The Natural.* The year was 1934 and Johnny Frederick had just set the record for most pinch–hit home runs in one year with six. It was to be Frederick's last year in the majors and, almost like bestowing a heirloom, he left the bat with his old Brooklyn Dodger teammate, Del Bissonette, who kept it in cold storage up in the attic of his Winthrop, Me. house. When Bissonette came back to coach and manage the Boston Braves in 1945, he exhumed Frederick's old bat and lent it to Braves star Tommy Holmes, who used it to set the then National League record for hitting in 37 consecutive games on his way to the home-run title.

NAME THE TWO MEN WHO HIT THE "ABE STARK" SIGN IN EBBETS FIELD.

A few years back, Joe Raposo wrote a song that sounded like a funeral dirge for a world that once was, the baseball world of the first two–plus decades of the twentieth century. The song, "There used to be a Ballpark," eulogizes a time that was and never will return, a time when the outfield walls were adorned with wonderful advertising signs offering free merchandise or cash to players who hit them. Perhaps the sign that has become most ingrained in baseballiana was the Bull Durham tobacco sign which promised players "$50 for hitting the Bull . . . with any fairly batted ball in a regularly scheduled game." It was a giant sign which usually stood in left field. Because those players, particularly pitchers, waiting to get into the game sat in the shadow of the outsized bull on the sign, the waiting area became ingrained into baseball parlance as the "bullpen." Other signs, like the Stoney's sign in Toronto's Maple Leaf Park ("Hit the Hole and Win $2,000 Cash") and the sign in Sacramento's Edward Field for a plumbing supply outfit ("Hit the Toilet Seat and Win $20) pockmarked old–time stadia everywhere, giving baseball a homey charm it has never recaptured.

Hank Greenberg remembers a sign put up by a local Greek restaurant that stood in right field when he first broke in at Beaumont, offering free "Dinners for a Month" to the first player hitting it. Greenberg, as slow afoot and he was powerful of bat, never expected to be the recipient of the restaurant's prize. But, on his first at–bat, he swung late on a fastball and, huffing and puffing, made it into third ahead of the wide throw with a triple. It was his first and only triple all season. According to Greenberg, "I ate better than anyone on the team, especially in those Depression days when no one had the money to buy a good meal."

Arguably the most famous of all such signs stood in Ebbets Field, built by a dealer in wrought iron. There, right beneath the right centerfield scoreboard, some 295 feet from homeplate, stood—or rather, crouched—something resembling a sign. The sign read, in letters barely visible to the naked eye, "Hit Sign/Win Suit." And beneath that offer was the name of the sponsor, "Abe Stark/1514 Pitkin Avenue" in letters that dominated the sign. Naturally, it's inaccessibility gave everyone a laugh, but none more so than George Price, who, in a delicious cartoon in *The New Yorker* satarized it by showing a sign of a similar nature for a cloak-and-suiter offering free merchandise to anyone hitting the smaller-than-small bull's eye. And there, poised behind the outfielder, glove at the ready, stood what was obviously a haberdasher, prepared to catch any ball getting by the outfielder—thereby saving himself the expense of having to give away a suit.

But Brooklyn outfielders needed no such help. From 1939 through 1947, the sentry posted by the Dodgers in right field to prevent the passage of any unauthorized ball was Dixie Walker, not only "The People's Cherce," but Abe Stark's as well. Despite unconfirmed reports that the sign had been reached by Mel Ott, Hack Wilson and Dolf Camilli amongst others, Walker repeatedly told his Dodger teamates that he "didn't recall anybody ever hitting the sign." A fact confirmed by Stark himself, who should have known, keeping a tight reign over his inventory of suits. Walker would then add, only half in jest, that he "hadn't even gotten a pair of slacks" for protecting the sign all those years. Walker's successor in right was Carl Furillo. If possible, Furillo not only saw Walker's accomplishments, but raised them one, hitting the sign himself. Known as "Snoonj,—a nickname given him by Arky Vaughan, who asked Furillo what a sign selling "*scungelli*" meant, and being told by Furillo they were "a snail delicacy that looks like a small ice cream cone"—Furillo played right field at the corner of the sign for right-handed hitters, "moving over to the line for lefties, with Snider coming over to cover the area." Furillo, who patroled that area for an even dozen years, saving "Abe Stark/1514 Pitkin Avenue" his entire summer stock with his shoe–string catches, remembers only two players ever hitting the sign, "Me and Ron Northey." And both had to be on the fly, no 'tweeners rolling between the outfielders and rolling to the fence need apply. Ever the spray-hitter, Furillo remembers his sign-nificant hit as "going over the head of Danny Litwhiler, who was playing me a little shallow." When he went to collect on the "Hit Sign/Win Suit" offer at "Abe Stark/1514 Pitkin Avenue," Furillo found "they didn't have what I wanted. But then I saw something in the showroom under the blue light," and selected what he thought was a light blue suit. However, like the old joke that has the haberdasher telling his prospective client, "You want a green suit?, Come over under the green light," Furillo found that "when I took the suit outside in the sunlight, it turned out to be gray." The suit had a career of 18 years, several years after Furillo's own had come unraveled. But then again, as they say in Brooklyn, he was "entituhled", one of only two men along with Ron Northey, ever to have gotten a suit from "Abe Stark/1514 Pitkin Avenue."

8th Inning
The Managers

WHO WERE THE ONLY TWO MANAGERS TO BE REPLACED WITH THEIR TEAMS IN FIRST PLACE?

Managing a major league club is much like walking a tight rope without a safety net. Casey Stengel, who did three years hard managing Brooklyn and then put in six years with the Braves in Boston where a cab driver who broke Casey's leg in a 1942 accident was voted, "Boston's Man of the Year," finally, like the contortionist, came into his own as manager of the New York Yankees. Casey's secret for success? "Keep the five guys who hate you away from the five who are undecided," he once said, a touch of ice water in his veins—tinged with V.O., of course.

But even Casey felt the slings and arrows of outrageous owners; he was fired by the Yankee owners after his team had faltered in the 1960 World Series, losing in seven games to Pittsburgh despite having the highest batting average of any World Series team in history.

Other managers have been replaced without ever having reached the pennant penthouse Stengel seemed to occupy on a permanent basis. Phil Cavaretta was fired in training camp, the only manager never to see opening day. And Eddie Sawyer left after a first–game loss in 1960, determined as he was"to live to see 50." But two managers did reach first place and were replaced for their efforts: Pat Corrales was given the boot by the Philadelphia Phillies in 1983 although his team was in first place in the National League East, albeit with a 43–42 record. His baton was turned over to Paul Owens, who brought the Phillies home in front and into the World Series before losing to the Baltimore Orioles.

Clyde Sukeforth was replaced as manager of the Brooklyn Dodgers in 1947 after the first game of the season, a win, and, not incidentally, Jackie Robinson's debut game. Sukeforth was a temporary replacement for the suspended Leo Durocher and was replaced in turn by Burt Shotton, who managed the rest of the year and took the Dodgers into the World Series, which they also lost to the New York Yankees.

WHO WAS THE ONLY MAN TO MANAGE TWO LAST–PLACE CLUBS IN ONE YEAR?

Since baseball immemorial, there have been but four managers who have either jumped or been pushed in midstream, starting the season with one club in one league and winding up with another club in the other league later on in the year. The four are: John McGraw (1902), Rogers Hornsby (1952), Bill Virdon (1975), and Pat Corrales (1983). But of the four, only McGraw, one of baseball's greatest managers, made managerial history of a sort, not to mention the Trivia Hall of Fame, by managing two last–place clubs in one year.

Known as "Little Napoleon" to his legion of fans, and by any name that came to mind to his detractors, all almost as picturesque as himself, McGraw made a giant leap of faith by jumping the Baltimore Orioles' sinking ship in midsummer of 1902 and crossing over to the National League and the New York Giants, debuting as manager and third baseman on July 19th. But McGraw didn't just leave the team; he took it with him, raiding the Baltimore franchise in the fledgling American League of many of its stars, including pitcher Joe McGinnity, catcher Roger Bresnahan, first baseman Dan McGann, and shortstop–second baseman Billy Gilbert. However, his transfusion didn't take, and the Giants still finished in eighth place, seven–and–one–half games behind the seventh–place Phillies. The Orioles, left to the temporary care of McGraw's old Oriole teammate and current business partner, Wilbert Robinson, floundered and also finished in eighth place, three–and–one–half games out of seventh. The next year found the Orioles and Wilbert Robinson in New York as well, with the Orioles becoming the New York Highlanders. However, Robinson, knowing which side of the base his butter was on, joined McGraw and his fellow expatriates as they made a run for the pennant, finishing second. By 1904 McGraw had accomplished what he set out to do, winning the National League pennant, his first of many. He also won his place in baseball history.

McGraw was to manage the Giants for 31 years, winning 10 pennants and three World Series those three–plus decades. When he finally retired, on June 3, 1932, he left baseball as the second winningest manager of all time. And he left the Giants in the same place they had been when he found them—last place.

WHAT MANAGER HAS THE MOST WINS WITHOUT EVER WINNING A PENNANT? WHAT MANAGER WITH THE LEAST WINS WON A PENNANT AND A WORLD SERIES?

Managing a baseball team is baseball's version of the last mile. From the day a manager is hired, he's also fired—the date just hasn't been filled in yet unless you're Connie Mack and own the team, which might explain why you were the manager with the mostest, 53 years, and 7,878 games. Besides Mack, the number who have managed for over 3,000 games, the equivalent of 20 years, can be counted on one's fingers. Literally. One of those, Gene Mauch, managed for 24 years and 3,617 games, and yet the best finish he ever fashioned was his first–place finish in the American League West in 1982. Unfortunately, Mauch's Angels lost the last three games of the American League championship series to the Milwaukee Brewers and Mauch was rewarded for his demipennant by being fired.

On the other side of the managerial coin, those managers who have won pennants with the leastest are two from back in the prehistoric era before 1900 (George Wright, 1871–1879; and Henry Lucas, 1884–1885) and one from the Federal League (Bill Phelphs, 1914–1915). But the manager with the least wins who has won a pennant and a World Series is George Dallas Green, who, in three years—from 1979 through the strike–shortened year of 1981—managed 301 games and won the pennant *and* the World Series of 1980.

WHO IS THE ONLY MAN TO BE SELECTED BOTH AS MANAGER OF THE YEAR AND ROOKIE OF THE YEAR?

Many of those who have won the Rookie of the Year Award since it was first initiated in 1947 have gone on to stardom and, for some, superstardom. But only seven of its recipients have ever gone on to manage major league teams: Alvin Dark (1948); Harvey Kuenn (1953); Bill Virdon (1955); Frank Robinson (1956); Frank Howard (1960); Pete Rose (1963); and, of more recent vintage, Lou Piniella (1969). And, of those five, only one, Bill Virdon, has been recognized by *The Sporting News* as the Manager of the Year, winning that designation in 1974 for bringing the New York Yankees home second in the American League East and in 1980 for winning the National League West with the Houston Astros. In managing the Yankees in 1974 and 1975, Virdon also gained another gold–leaf cluster on his Trivia Hall of Fame plaque; he was the only Yankee manager since 1923 *not* to manage the Yankees in Yankee Stadium, his year–plus tenure coming during the stadium's renovation so that his charges played their home games at crosstown Shea Stadium. Ironically, it was while he was serving as keeper–of–the–shrine, that Virdon was fired by Yankee boss George Steinbrenner in midseason 1975 and found himself on the Astros for their last 34 games—one of the only four managers to manage in both leagues in the same year, still a third distinction for the only man to be selected both as Manager of the Year and Rookie of the Year.

WHAT MANAGER REMOVED TWO PITCHERS IN THE EIGHTH INNING WHILE BOTH WERE PITCHING NO–HITTERS?

Pitching for the San Diego Padres against the New York Mets on July 21, 1970, Clay Kirby found himself in the middle of a no–hit effort after eight innings. But in the bottom of the eighth, manager Preston Gomez pulled Kirby for a pinch hitter and the Mets got a hit in the ninth off Kirby's reliever to win the game. Four years later, on September 4, 1974, Don Wilson, the Houston Astros' ace, found himself in much the same situation, having pitched eight innings of no–hit ball. But Wilson too was lifted for a pinch hitter in the bottom of the eighth and his once somnolent opponents, the Cincinnati Reds, suddenly found his reliever's offerings more to their liking and broke up the no-hitter in the ninth. The manager of the Houston Astros at the time was the same Preston Gomez who was consistent, even if not correct, in his strategy.

WHO IS THE ONLY MANAGER WHO, AS A PLAYER, HIT A HOME RUN ON THE VERY FIRST PITCH HE EVER SAW IN THE MAJORS?

There is no achievement in the whole of baseball that can compare, both for its economy of effort and its efficiency of result, with the hitting of a home run on the very first pitch a player sees in the major leagues. Not only is it an impossible act to follow, but for some of those who have climbed that rare mountain and smelled its rarified atmosphere, it's all downhill from there—a fact borne out by Bill LeFebvre who hit a home run on the first pitch he ever saw back in 1938, his only time at bat in his rookie year, never to hit another during his four–year career.

The first of the 10 men who have hit home runs on the first

pitch they ever saw was Clise Dudley, a pitcher for the Brooklyn Dodgers, who smote the first pitch he ever saw from Claude Willoughby out of that little bandbox known as Baker's Bowl, baseball's answer to fallen arches, on April 27, 1929.

The nine others who have accomplished this rare feat are, in order: Eddie Morgan, Bill LeFebvre, Clyde Vollmer, George Vico, Chuck Tanner, Bert Campaneris, Brant Alyea, Don Rose, and Gary Gaetti. And of this small group of men who have had one split second of baseball immortality, only one, Chuck Tanner—who hit his first–pitch home run off Gerry Staley on April 12, 1955—went on to become a Major League manager, joining Whitey Lockman as one of the only two men who have hit a home run in their first at–bat to later become managers. Lockman, however, was not quite as efficient as Tanner. He took his time, as well as a couple of pitches, to hit a home run in his first at–bat in the majors.

WHEN WAS THE ONLY TIME IN MAJOR LEAGUE HISTORY THAT TWO PLAYING MANAGERS PITCHED AGAINST EACH OTHER?

Since the advent of baseball, the number of pitchers who have become managers totals 40, the least–represented position in the managerial ranks. More than a few of those managers have gone to success, if not greatness, in their new careers—Tommy Lasorda, Bob Lemon, and Dallas Green all winning pennants and World Series after their playing careers were over and others, like Walter Johnson and Clark Griffith, possessing managerial won–lost records far above .500. In fact, dating back to A. G. Spalding, who served as pitcher–manager of the Chicago entry in the original National League and won the first National League game in history, a 4–0 victory over Louisville in 1876, several managers have also been pitching managers. The aforementioned Clark Griffith won the most games for himself as manager, a total of 68 over seven years. However, almost as if it were a multiple–choice question answer, none of the above faced each other as managers, but two others. And those two others were not pitchers, by any stretch of the imagination, but great batsmen: Ty Cobb and George Sisler. These two greats, then serving as playing–managers of the Detroit Tigers and St. Louis Browns, respectively, agreed to meet on the afternoon of October 4, 1925, the last day of the season for their third–and fourth–place teams. The two had already hooked up once before, when neither was manager, back on September 1, 1918, again the last day of that foreshortened year, with Cobb pitching two innings in relief and Sisler one—Sisler getting a double off Cobb to compound the felony. Now, two distinguished stars in an undistinguished game, the two again faced each other. Again, as relief pitchers. This time around Cobb pitched one perfect inning and Sisler two scoreless innings in an 11–6 win for Detroit—the only time in baseball history two playing–managers have ever pitched against each other.

WHAT MANAGER RESIGNED THE DAY FOUR HOME RUNS WERE HIT?

The accounts of managers' comings and goings would fill a 26–volume encyclopedia; the rendering of those hitting four home runs in a game could be placed in the navel of a flea with enough room left over for those hitting three in a game. However, one time these two ledgers did come in contact. For, on June 3, 1932, John McGraw retired as manager of the New York Giants after a run of 31 years, while Lou Gehrig, who was accustomed to playing second fiddle, had to do it one more time, his four home runs gaining coverage in the New York papers right under the shipping news. Gehrig, resigned to his fate of second banana, merely muttered, "I guess I'm just not a headline player."

NAME THE ONLY FATHER–SON COMBINATION TO MANAGE IN THE MAJOR LEAGUES.

Managing a Major League team is not something to be handed down like an heirloom, obviously, there having been only one father–son tandem ever to manage in the big leagues—the Sislers, George and Dick. *Père* George managed three years, 1924 through 1926, leading the St. Louis Browns to a fourth–place, third–place and seventh–place finish and 218 wins in 459 games for a .475 won-lost record. His son, Dick, managing the Cincinnati Reds for parts of two seasons, 1964 and 1965, wound up with a 121–94 won-lost record, bringing the Sisler family record to a total of 339 and 335, a shade over the .500 mark. One manager, conversely, worked for both a father and a son team: Rogers Hornsby, who managed the Chicago Cubs under Bill Veeck, Sr., and the St. Louis Browns under his son, Bill Veeck, Jr.

WHAT PLAYER HAD THE LONGEST CAREER IN THE MAJORS UNDER ONLY ONE MANAGER?

Stability has never been one of baseball's long suits. Many's the player who has had his hand dealt to him, only to find it quickly reshuffled. One such player was Tony Curry, who came up with the Phillies in 1960 and had the unusual experience of playing for three managers in his first three games in the majors: Eddie Sawyer, who started the season and quit after one game, interim manager Andy Cohen, who stayed for exactly one game; and, finally, Gene Mauch, who stayed the remainder of the year—and eight years more. Another who had the impression that managers were changed every road trip was Cy Williams, who, during his 19–year career had a total of 14 managers, including 12 in his first 12 years in the major leagues. But the all–time record for managerial instability belongs to Deacon Jim McGuire, who, during his 26–year–career, played for 23 different managers, one of whom was Deacon Jim McGuire.

Contrasted with these manager–a–minute players is Don Drysdale who played his entire 14–year career under one manager, Walter Alston. Other players like Eddie Plank and Christy Mathewson played for Connie Mack and John McGraw for 14 and 15 years, respectively, but ended their careers under other managers, leaving Drysdale as the player who had the longest major league career under only one manager.

9th Inning
The Teams

WHICH MAJOR LEAGUE TEAM DID NOT HAVE A SINGLE PLAYER ON ITS ROSTER WITH AT LEAST 100 HITS?

The two most impotent teams in baseball history are reputed to have been the 1942 Philadelphia Phillies and the 1916 Philadelphia A's, two teams that can be called teams only in the same way raisins are called fruits, technically and only in a manner of speaking. Their talent was threadbare, undistinguished, and uninspiring. They led their league in negative categories: most losses, fewest hits, fewest runs scored, highest earned run averages, most bases on balls surrendered by their pitching staffs, and totally anemic efforts, finishing 18½ and 40 games out of seventh place, respectively but not respectfully. But despite their inept performances, both teams had at least four players with 100 or more hits on their rosters. It remained for the 1972 New York Mets, a team then just one year away from the National

League pennant, to claim the dubious distinction of having been the only major league club in a *full* season (discounting the Toronto Blue Jays in the strike–shortened season of 1981) to fail to have at least one player on its roster with 100 hits.

WHAT TEAM HAD THE ONLY ALL SWITCH–HITTING INFIELD IN BASEBALL HISTORY?

Switch–hitting was a rare commodity in the early days of baseball. But by the 1903 World Series it had become something more of a curiosity than a rarity, two of the participants—Candy LaChance of the Red Sox and Claude Ritchey of the Pirates—hitting from both sides of the plate. Down through the years the trickle of switch–hitters turned into a Niagara. By 1965 the Los Angeles Dodgers had capped the phenomenon by fielding the only all switch–hitting infield in baseball history: Wes Parker at first, Jim Lefebvre at second, Maury Wills at short, and Junior Gilliam at third. For a brief period in 1971, the St. Louis Cardinals held a special niche on the all switch–hitting something–or–other team, boasting a catching staff that had two switch–hitting catchers, Bob Stinson joining Ted Simmons for 17 games behind the plate.

WHAT WAS THE ONLY TEAM IN BASEBALL HISTORY TO WIN A CHAMPIONSHIP OF ANY SORT THAT ALLOWED MORE RUNS THAN THEY SCORED?

One of the criteria that is supposedly needed for winning a pennant, let alone a game, is to outscore the opponent. But, according to baseball's statistical guru, Bill James, once, just once, in an impersonation of the Flying Wallendas, a team was outscored over the entire season by its opponents and still managed to win a championship. The team? The Kansas City Royals of 1984, which won the Western Division of the American League despite being outscored by 13 runs over a 162–game schedule, 673 to 686. Not surprisingly they were outscored in the American League championship series by Detroit in all three games that fall as well. But, like the 1979 Phillies who also were outscored, they came back the following year, again like the Phillies, to win the World Series.

WHAT WAS THE LAST ALL–WHITE TEAM TO WIN A PENNANT?

The year 1947—when Jackie Robinson entered the majors—marks for baseball what Anno Domini marks for the Christian era. And yet, despite the pioneering of some managers, such as Branch Rickey and Bill Veeck, others, whose broad minds had changed places with their thin waists, held out against the change. The Boston Red Sox, for instance, kept their colors red and Caucasian until 1959. One of the last teams to incorporate a black into its roster was the New York Yankees, who, in 1953, became the last all–white team to win a pennant. And when that black Yankee finally arrived in the person of Elston Howard—obvious choices in the minors like Suitcase Simpson and Vic

Power had been bypassed—Casey Stengel, with tongue swelling noticably in his cheeck, said, as an aside, "When I finally get a nigger, I get the only one who can't run."

WHEN WAS THE ONLY TIME IN BASEBALL HISTORY BOTH PENNANT WINNERS HAD THE EXACT SAME NUMBER OF WINS, LOSSES, PERCENTAGE, AND WINNING MARGIN OVER THE SECOND–PLACE FINISHER?

With all the permutations conceivable for pennant winners—wins, losses, and winning margin—it is almost inconceivable that two teams could finish with the exact same record in the same year. Almost, but not quite, as the 1949 New York Yankees and the 1949 Brooklyn Dodgers both finished with a 97–57 record for a .630 won–lost percentage, one game ahead of the Boston Red Sox and St. Louis Cardinals who both finished with 96–58 records.

WHAT WAS THE YOUNGEST TEAM EVER TO TAKE THE FIELD IN A MAJOR LEAGUE GAME?

The all–time peach fuzz team took the field for the Houston Colt .45s on the night of Friday, September 27, 1963 to face the New York Mets. The team, comprised of nine rookies, averaged nineteen years and four months, younger by far than the previous playerlings, the wartime 1942 St. Louis Cardinals, who were the booty of any scout who could lasso, corral, or throw a net over any toilet–trained child or Spanish-American War veteran who had once played alongside the likes of Hugh Duffy and Wee Willie Keeler.

The team of rookies that Houston manager Harry Craft crayoned in the lineup card that night included: First base, Rusty Staub, 19 years old; Second base, Joe Morgan, 20; Shortstop, Sonny Jackson, 19; Third base, Glenn Vaughan, 19; Outfield, Jim Wynn, 21; Aaron Pointer, 21; and Brock Davis, 19; Catcher, Jerry Grote, 20; and Pitcher, Jay Dahl, 17, in his only major league appearance. The Colts were to lose the game that night to the Mets 10–3. But even more tragic was the fact that Dahl would perish before his 20th birthday in an auto accident, the youngest major league player ever to die.

WHAT WAS THE ONLY TIME A MAJOR LEAGUE TEAM, BOTH INDIVIDUALLY AND AS A TEAM, EMERGED FROM A GAME WITH THE SAME BATTING AVERAGE THEY BEGAN WITH?

The pitching sensation of the 1939 season was a 20–year–old fireballer out of Van Meter, Ia., nicknamed "Rapid Robert" as in "Rapid Robert" Feller. Feller had led the American League in victories, complete games, innings pitched, strikeouts, and shutouts. He now seemed to be on the cusp of real greatness as the 1940 season started. His first pitching assignment came on Tuesday, April 16, Opening Day in 1940 against the Chicago White Sox at Chicago's Comisky Park. The by–now 21–year–old version of the younger "Rapid Robert" pitched like a painter, laying down new coat upon new coat with his every pitch, and added to his luster by pitching the first of his three no–hitters that afternoon against the ChiSox. He struck out eight and walked five in setting the White Sox down without a hit, leaving both the individual batters and the entire team with the exact same batting average as the one they had just hours before when the 1940 season started that April 16th day.—.000.

WHICH TEAM HAD THE MOST MOST VALUABLE PLAYERS ON ITS ROSTER?

The Most Valuable Player Award was an outgrowth of an award made in 1910 by the Chalmers Motor Car Co., which offered its most expensive touring car, the Chalmers 30, to the batting champion of the major leagues—the first sports award ever given out for product publicity. But no sooner had they announced their award then the Chalmers Co. became embroiled in a controversy. For by midseason it had become apparent to all that the car would go to the American League batting champion, its leading batsmen hitting more than 50 points higher than those in the National League. Anything beyond that was uncertain while the two contenders for the Chalmers 30, Cleveland's Nap Lajoie and Detroit's Ty Cobb, continued to exchange the lead on a day–to–day basis. With but two weeks to go, Lajoie led Cobb by a mere four points, .375 to .371. Cobb was riding the bench because of an inflammation of the eye when Lajoie went on a hitting spree, collecting 23 hits in 10 games to push his average up to .380. Returning to the lineup, Cobb went seven for 13 before the eye flared up again, forcing him to sit out the last two games of the year with a by–now average of .385. With two games remaining for him to take the Chalmers away from Cobb, Lajoie went into St. Louis where the Hate Cobb faction of the American League did its best to hand–deliver the Chalmers to the Cleveland slugger. On orders from their manager, Jack O'Connor, the Browns played Lajoie back—far back, halfway to Joplin—allowing Lajoie to beat out seven infield bunts and convert a short outfield fly into a triple for a total of eight hits. But even though the Chicago *Tribune* statisticians gave the batting title to Lajoie, .385 to .381, when the official tabulations came out they read, Cobb .3848 and Lajoie .3841, a margin of seven one-thousandths of a percentage point. This result was slightly tainted by the discovery some 65 years later by the Society of American Baseball Research (SABR) and first chronicled in the 1978 book *Hit the Sign and Win a Free Suit of Clothes from Harry Finklestein* which showed that one of Cobb's 2–for–3 days had been double–counted by the American League office, and that his average, without the more–than–compensatory help from the league, was in reality .383, a thousandth of a point less than Lajoie's.

The Chalmers Motor Car Co., glad for the publicity but relieved that their travail was over, gave both players automobiles in the interest of good publicity—which is what it had been about since the beginning of the promotion. The next year, determined not to get caught in the same promotional gridlock, the Chalmers Co. resculptured its award, their car going to the player deemed by the baseball writers to be "most valuable to a team in his league." This was the first such Most–Valuable–Player Award, one given to Frank Schulte of the Chicago Cubs and Ty Cobb in 1911. After 1914 the Chalmers Co. discontinued the award, and soon discontinued itself. But the award was reinstated in 1922 by the leagues, this time with $1,000 in gold coins not only going with the trophy, but inserted into the trophy itself. And when the league dropped its award in 1929, the Baseball Writers Association picked it up on its second bounce, reinstating it in 1931 and carrying it through until today.

During the times the Most Valuable Player Award has been given, there have been no less than 105 winners. And yet, one team, the 1933 Cardinals, once boasted of having seven winners—past, present, and future—on its roster in the persons of Jim Bottomley, Dizzy Dean, Frankie Frisch, Rogers Hornsby, Joe Medwick, Bob O'Farrell, and Dazzy Vance, one helluva gathering of talent for a team that finished in fifth place, and the most Most Valuable Players of any team in history.

WHEN WAS THE ONLY TIME ALL OF THE MANAGERS IN ONE LEAGUE WERE PLAYING MANAGERS?

It was back in 1969, and two of the denizens of the Cubbie Bear Bar, cattycornered across the street from Wrigley Field, were discussing the sad plight of the '69 Cubs when another of the locals stepped in with, "Did ya hear that they're moving the Cubs to the Philippines next year? Yeah, they're gonna call 'em the 'Manilla Folders.'" Team nicknames have always been part of the baseball tradition, even if some of them have sounded like they were the losing entries in a name–the–team contest. Or worse. Take the names of the Federal League teams. Please. Those teams which entered baseball in 1914 in a misguided attempt to share in what was envisioned as baseball's great and expanding horizon were: the Indiana Hoosiers, the Chicago Whales, the Baltimore Terrapins, the Buffalo Blues, the Brooklyn Tip Tops, the Kansas City Packers, the Pittsburgh Rebels, the St. Louis Terriers and the Newark Peppers (1915's version of the 1914 Indiana Hoosiers). It was in the same 1915 season, the Federal League's last gasp, that the owners, despairing of their payrolls, decided to double up the duties of some of their high–priced talent in an effort to stave off the inevitable. Each of the eight Federal League teams pressed into managerial duty one of its players—the Chicago Whales, Joe Tinker; the Baltimore Terrapins, Otto Knable; the Buffalo Blues, Harry Lord; the Brooklyn Tip Tops, Lee Magee; the Kansas City Packers, George Stovall; the Pittsburgh Rebels, Rebel Oakes; the St. Louis Terriers, Fielder Jones; and the Newark Peppers, Bill McKechnie—to field the only all–league all–playing-manager team. This was the only time in baseball history that every manager was a player. And vice versa.

WHICH TEAM'S INFIELD PLAYED TOGETHER THE LONGEST?

Most infields look as if they're the same set of characters, constantly appearing and reappearing as if part of a repertory company, merely playing different parts. But every now and then an infield becomes set, put in place almost as if by super glue. One such infield was the famed Tinker–Evers–Chance combination with third base handled by Harry Steinfeldt after short tries with Germany Schaefer and Doc Casey didn't take. There was Connie Mack's famed $100,000 Infield with Home Run Baker at third, Stuffy McInnis at first, and Jack Barry and Eddie Collins the pulse beat at short and second. And there was the famed infield that peppered the Gas House Gang Cardinal squad of 1934, a cast of characters starring Pepper Martin, Leo Durocher, Frankie Frisch, and Rip Collins. There have even been great batting infields, like the three infields since 1900 where all four men have hit .300—the 1926 Giants of Kelly, Frisch, Jackson, and Lindstrom, the 1927 Giants of Terry, Hornsby, Jackson, and Lindstrom, and the 1930 Cardinals foursome of Bottomley, Frisch, Gelbert, and Adams. But none of these units have had the longest careers playing together. The honor for the infield that played together and stayed together longest goes to the Los Angeles Dodgers infield from 1974 through 1981, a fearsome foursome made up of Steve Garvey at first base, Davey Lopes at second base, Bill Russell at shortstop, and Ron Cey at third base. The foursome was only broken up when Steve Sax—whom one wag suggested wore a glove on his left hand for the same reason Michael Jackson wore one on his left, for no apparent reason—replaced Lopes. Together these four played together for eight–plus years, beating out the previous longest–running—and throwing—infield, the Chicago White Stockings' Stonewall Infield that played together from 1883 through 1889.

NAME THE ONLY TIME TWO TEAMMATES ON A WORLD'S CHAMPIONSHIP TEAM FINISHED ONE–TWO IN BATTING.

There is no second prize for the runners–up in either war or in the quest for a batting title. But several times the runner–up has been almost as notable as the winner, as when, in 1966, Matty Alou beat out his brother, Felipe, for the National League batting title. Or, in the case where the two leading batsmen are teammates, something that has happened a total of 24 times in baseball history. However, these cases of team quinellas have only occurred three times on pennant winners—the 1903 Pirates, when Honus Wagner outdistanced Fred Clarke; the 1907 Tigers, when Ty Cobb beat out Sam Crawford; and the 1908 Tigers, when Crawford again finished second to Cobb—and only once on a World's Championship team: in 1954, when Willie Mays hit .345 to lead the league, barely beating out teammate Don Mueller, who hit .342.

TEAMMATES, 1–2 IN LEAGUE–LEADING BATTING AVERAGES

1880—George Gore, .360; Cap Anson, .337—Chicago, NL
1884—Fred Dunlap, .412; Orator Shaffer, .360—St. Louis Union
1886—King Kelly, .388; Cap Anson, .371—Chicago, NL
1886—Guy Hecker, .342; Pete Browning, .340—Louisville, American Association
1888—Cap Anson, .344; Jimmy Ryan, .332—Chicago, NL
*1891—Dan Brouthers, .350; Hugh Duffy, .336—Boston, American Association
*1893—Billy Hamilton, .380; Sam Thompson, .370—Philadelphia, NL
1903—Honus Wagner, .355; Fred Clarke, .351—Pittsburgh, NL
1907—Ty Cobb, .350; Sam Crawford, .323—Detroit, AL
1908—Ty Cobb, .324; Sam Crawford, .311—Detroit, AL
1919—Ty Cobb, .384; Bobby Veach, .355—Detroit, AL
1921—Harry Heilmann, .394; Ty Cobb, .389—Detroit, AL
1923—Rogers Hornsby, .384; Jim Bottomley, .371—St. Louis, NL
1925—Rogers Hornsby, .403; Jim Bottomley, .367—St. Louis, NL
1926—Bubbles Hargrave, .353; Cuckoo Christensen, .350—Cincinnati, NL
1937—Joe Medwick, .374; Johnny Mize, .364—St. Louis, NL
1942—Ted Williams, .356; Johnny Pesky, .331—Boston, AL

*Teammate also finishing third in batting

1954—Willie Mays, .354; Don Mueller, .342—New York, NL
1958—Ted Williams, .388; Pete Runnels, .322—Boston, AL
1959—Harvey Kuenn, .353; Al Kaline, .327—Detroit, AL
1961—Norm Cash, .361; Al Kaline, .324—Detroit, AL
1976—George Brett, .333; Hal McRae, .332—Kansas City, AL
1977—Rod Carew, .388; Lyman Bostock, .336—Minnesota, AL
1984—Don Mattingly, .343; Dave Winfield, .340—New York, AL

WHAT TWO TEAMS WERE INVOLVED IN THE MOST EVENLY PLAYED GAME IN MAJOR LEAGUE HISTORY?

There have been three tie games played in World Series history. The first was the initial game of the 1907 Series between the Tigers and the Cubs—a 3–3 tie, called on account of darkness. Before the game the Tigers' Germany Schaefer had asked one of the league officials, "What happens if it's a 'tie'?" prompting the league office to refund all proceeds. In the second game of the 1912 Series and in the second game of the 1921 Series the receipts were also turned over, this time to charity by the irate commissioner. All three times the reason given for the final tie was "darkness." But since lights were first introduced in 1935, that basis for calling a game has been removed, to be supplanted by others—such as rain or curfew. However, in most cases, those games called are normally only suspended, to be concluded at a later date.

However, there was one game that was called, "on account of darkness" that remains the most evenly played game in baseball history: the second game of a Saturday double-header played at Brooklyn's Washington Park between the Brooklyn Dodgers and the Pittsburgh Pirates. Called after nine innings, the game stood 8–8. It was symmetrical in other ways as well. Mirror-like statistics for both teams included 38 at-bats for both, eight runs for both, 27 put-outs for both, and 12 assists for both. Moreover, with every player trying to get into the act, it began to take on the look of a "Twelve Lords aleaping game," with each side having two pitchers (Rucker and Dessau for Brooklyn, Camnitz and Leever for Pittsburgh), with each pair of pitchers giving up eqqual totals of 13 hits, five strikeouts, one hit batsman and three walks. Each side's catcher (George Gibson of Pittsburgh and Tex Erwin of Brooklyn) having one passed ball, six put-outs, one assist, four at–bats, one hit and no runs; each second baseman—Dots Miller of Pittsburgh and Silent John Hummel of Brooklyn—having two hits and two runs apiece; each of the shortstops—Honus Wagner of Pittsburgh and Pryor McElveen of Brooklyn—having two singles and no runs; each right fielder—the Pirate's Chief Wilson and Brooklyn's Jack Dalton—having one put out, five at–bats and two hits apiece; each center fielder—Tommy Leach of the Pirates and Bill Davidson of the Dodgers—having five at–bats and two put outs each; and each first baseman—John Flynn of Pittsburgh and Jake Daubert of Brooklyn—having four at–bats and one run each. It was a game like no other game in baseball history—a "tie" in every sense of the word.

WHAT TEAM HAS HAD THE MOST PLAYERS WIN BATTING TITLES?

During baseball's Brotherhood War of 1890—a war that is about as memorable as Shay's Rebellion—the Philadelphia Athletics, who had recently been rejoined by several of their players who had jumped their claims more times than an Alaskan panhandler, inadvertently left the names of two of their players off their club rosters. When one of them, Louis Bierbauer, jumped again to join the Pittsburg club, the Athletics protested the actions of the Pittsburghers as "Piratical," a name which was picked up by the less-than-imaginative sportswriters of the era and made "Pirates." Throughout the following 95 years of their existence, the Pirates have not so much preyed on other teams than their batters have preyed on other pitchers with no less than 10 of their members winning the National League batting championship a total of 24 times: Honus Wagner, 1900, 1903, 1904, 1906, 1907, 1908, 1909 and 1911; Ginger Beaumont, 1902; Paul Waner, 1928, 1934 and 1936; Arky Vaughn, 1935; Debs Garms, 1940; Dick Groat, 1960; Roberto Clemente, 1961, 1964, 1965, and 1967; Matty Alou, 1966; Dave Parker, 1977 and 1978; Bill Madlock, 1981 and 1983.